Who Is Jesus Christ?

D1566961

Steven W. Mosher
Population Research Institute
P. O. Box 1559
Front Royal, VA 22630

Who Is Jesus Christ?

Unlocking
the Mystery
in the Gospel
of Matthew

Eric Sammons

Our Sunday Visitor Publishing Division
Our Sunday Visitor, Inc.
Huntington, Indiana 46750

Cover design by Rebecca J. Heaston
Cover image: Shutterstock
Interior design by Siok-Tin Sodbinow

PRINTED IN THE UNITED STATES OF AMERICA

Endorsements for

Who Is Jesus Christ? Unlocking the Mystery in the Gospel of Matthew
by Eric Sammons

Our Holy Father, Pope Benedict XVI, in his reflections on the 2008 Synod on the Word of God, taught us that "Coming into communion with the Word of God, we enter a communion of the Church that lives the Word of God." Eric Sammons' reflections examine the titles and names given to Jesus by those who knew him, as recorded in the Gospel of Saint Matthew. Drawing on his own faith journey and his personal experience, Eric Sammons demonstrates how the lived Word of God — reflected in the lives and writings of the saints and prayers of the Church — of both the East and West — can help us to better know Jesus and to strive to form our daily lives into his likeness. *Who Is Jesus Christ? Unlocking the Mystery in the Gospel of Matthew* is a work of devotion and readers should find it both inspiring and encouraging.

— Most Reverend Donald W. Wuerl, S.T.D.,
Archbishop of Washington

Using vivid examples and a clear, accessible style, Sammons illuminates for readers the portrait of Jesus that is presented in the Gospel of Matthew. This book is filled with striking insights that make the Gospel come alive. Readers will find their understanding of Jesus and how he fulfills the Old Testament profoundly enriched by Sammons' work. This volume exemplifies what the world Synod of Bishops recently called for: sound biblical resources that help people encounter Christ, the Word made flesh, in the reading of Scripture.

— Mary Healy, Ph.D., General Editor, *Catholic Commentary on Sacred Scripture*

Eric Sammons knows how to cut to the chase with grace and aplomb. *Who Is Jesus Christ?* is the most important question that has ever been asked in the history of the human race and he ably helps us answer it — and all the deepest longings of the human heart — through the Christ he serves so well.

— Mark P. Shea, Author, *Mary: Mother of the Son*

I am happy to recommend Eric Sammons' book *Who Is Jesus Christ? Unlocking the Mystery in the Gospel of Matthew.* Eric has chosen as his topic meeting Jesus in the Gospel of Matthew. He proceeds by using Scripture to understand Scripture, seeing the Word of God as a whole as the Church has always done. He uses modern insights, those of the Fathers of the Church, the timeless teaching of the Church as well as his own, born of prayerful reading and study. In all this he is in the grand tradition of *Lectio Divina* recently discussed by the Bishops of the world in synod assembled. Those who read this book will be richly rewarded as they seek to encounter the Lord in Matthew's Gospel.

— Fr. Giles R. Dimock, O.P., S.T.D., Prior,
Dominican House of Studies

This book presents an excellent survey of key images of Jesus of Nazareth, Son of God, as presented in St. Matthew's Gospel. It establishes St. Matthew's historical and theological understandings of Jesus in his original setting and then draws from Sacred Tradition in order to lead the reader into deep spiritual and theological waters. The uniqueness of this book is in consideration of central Christological terms as well as other ascriptions given to Jesus (e.g., "ghost," "man," "carpenter's son"). The net effect is a very rich presentation of the many dimensions of Jesus as seen from many Gospel perspectives. This well-written book is a very rich presentation of Jesus suitable for adult study groups in parishes, senior high school classes, and introductory college-level courses.

— Stephen F. Miletic, Ph.D., Professor of Sacred Scripture,
Franciscan University of Steubenville

Contents

For Suzan

Acknowledgments

I am grateful beyond measure to all those who had a hand in the writing and publication of this book.

I want to thank Fr. Conrad Osterhaut, Fr. Giles Dimock, Jim Kruggel, Mary Healy, Dean Austin, and most of all, Lisa Sharafinski for their valuable comments during the editing process of the book.

Thanks also to Fr. Benedict Groeschel for writing the foreword and for the wonderful work for the poor and the unborn he and all the Franciscan Friars of the Renewal have done over the years.

Thank you to Bert Ghezzi and all the fine folks at Our Sunday Visitor for making this book more than just a stack of paper on my bookshelf.

I am especially indebted to all those heroes of the faith who have gone before us and have read, interpreted, and lived the Scriptures for generation after generation, particularly St. Matthew, St. Paul, Origen, St. Athanasius, St. John Chrysostom, St. Augustine, and St. Jerome. Without them, our understanding of the Scriptures would be much poorer.

I am grateful to my children, Anna, Lucy, Maria, and Peter, for their enthusiastic support and their patience during the writing process. Furthermore, I'm happy that my youngest daughter, Hope, waited until I turned in my manuscript to be born!

Finally, I want to thank my wife and editor, Suzan. No one would have wanted to see what this book was like before she took her red pen to it. Little did I know when I married her that not only would she be a wonderful wife and mother but also quite adept at spotting dangling participles and poor grammatical constructions. God has given me many good gifts, but none better than her!

FOREWORD

As I read *Who Is Jesus Christ? Unlocking the Mystery in the Gospel of Matthew,* it seemed to me that I was in the presence of someone who was hard at work on the creation of a beautiful mosaic or an exquisite tapestry. In this book, Eric Sammons presents us with a fascinating and truthful picture of our Lord Jesus Christ. It is a picture he fashions for us step by slow step from material found primarily in the Gospel of St. Matthew, but with fitting additions taken from other parts of Holy Scripture, both the Old and New Testaments, and from many writers in the Catholic tradition as well. In my opinion, Sammons' book is an excellent example of canonical exegesis, which Pope Benedict called for in his own book, *Jesus of Nazareth.* The pope tells us:

> "Canonical exegesis"—reading the individual texts of the Bible in the context of the whole — is an essential dimension of exegesis. It does not contradict historical-critical interpretation but carries it forward in an organic way toward becoming theology in the proper sense. [i]

For the informed and educated reader who wishes the kind of biblical study that opens the door to real theology, Eric Sammons' book is worth the serious effort that is needed to read it.

I suggest that no one read this book quickly, for although it is not lengthy, it contains a great deal of information as well as many opportunities for prayer and meditation. I also suggest that the reader delve into one chapter at a time, preferably with a copy of the Bible on hand. Eric Sammons has not written the kind of book you can pick up and put down, simply picking up where you left off at some later time. He has written instead a careful and

---

[i] Joseph Ratzinger, Pope Benedict XVI, *Jesus of Nazareth* (New York: Doubleday, 2007), p. XIX.

thoughtful study that requires the reader to approach it with the same care with which it was written. If you do this, you will be greatly rewarded. Working through Sammons' book is like taking a course by a well-informed and highly intelligent teacher. At the same time, it is like making a retreat led by a prayerful and spiritual retreat master.

The subject, of course, is of the greatest interest. What can be more important than a deeper understanding of Jesus Christ? Unfortunately, in recent decades, the figure of Our Lord has been blurred and even obscured. This has come about for many reasons, but primary among them is the type of scholarship to which the Gospels were subjected for much of the twentieth century. Again, Pope Benedict has been very clear in his criticism of this type of scholarship, the historical-critical method and other related methods. He points out that alone they are inadequate and likely to produce a figure of Christ that is too remote and unknowable. The pope tells us that this approach to biblical studies has produced the mistaken impression that little certain knowledge of Jesus can be found, and that this impression has wrongly entered the minds of Christians, limiting their understanding of Christ. Concerning this, he writes:

> This is a dramatic situation for faith, because its point of reference is being placed in doubt: Intimate friendship with Jesus, on which everything depends, is in danger of clutching at thin air. [ii]

This is certainly the case. Many Christians today are no longer even sure they know who Jesus of Nazareth really is.

Sammons' work is a very serious and well-thought-out attempt to teach us, once again, just who is being proclaimed in the Gospel of St. Matthew. It is a slow, steady journey through this Gospel, a journey that pauses over and over again to examine, in a thoughtful and prayerful way, the names and titles given to our Lord in this

---

[ii] Ibid., p. XII.

Gospel. In each name we find something significant. Every title, we learn, offers us a slightly different way to look at Christ, a new prism through which to see him. What we glean from each name or title contributes to the total picture of our Savior, a picture that gradually becomes clearer and clearer until it is luminous.

Beginning with the pope himself, the effort to present the faithful with an adequate picture of Christ is well underway. It is an effort well supported by Eric Sammons. I hope that in years to come, he will follow this book up with later volumes on the other evangelists. I also hope that we will see more and more books like this, intelligent and erudite, yet accessible, on our Divine Savior and his life and personality. It is time to reject and reverse the influence of writers like Rudolf Bultmann, who dismantled the picture of Christ, leaving us only with remnants. In the place of such destruction we now have books like *Who Is Jesus Christ? Unlocking the Mystery in the Gospel of Matthew* — books that rebuild or, rather, reveal anew the true picture of Christ.

— Fr. Benedict J. Groeschel, C.F.R.

INTRODUCTION

The young college student boarded the subway heading for her internship in downtown Washington, DC, just as she had every day that summer. Following her now-typical routine, she squeezed into the crowded train for the half-hour ride to her office and opened her small Gideon Bible to the Gospels. Twenty years of Sunday Masses had given her a certain familiarity with the stories of the Bible, especially the accounts of the life of Jesus. Yet for some reason, in these months something was different. Instead of rehashing lifeless tales, she was discovering beautiful details about our Lord that she had never perceived. Whereas before the Gospels were dry narratives floating somewhere in the back of her consciousness, now the inspired words of Scripture leapt off the small pages and entered her heart. In a summer of grace, she was changed forever as she unlocked the mysteries of Scripture and encountered Christ in those sacred pages.

This true story reflects the power of the Bible, and especially of the Gospels, to lead us into an encounter with Christ that changes our lives. The inspired Word of God can lead us to a direct experience with the incarnate Word of God. It is "living and active, sharper than any two-edged sword, piercing to the division of soul and spirit, of joints and marrow, and discerning the thoughts and intentions of the heart" (Heb 4:12). But too often our reading of the Bible becomes stale and ineffective, leading us nowhere. Our initially exciting reading of the Sacred Word wanes over the years into a monotonous routine. How often have we heard the Word of God proclaimed in our churches and forgotten the words two minutes later? How often do we read a passage from our Bibles without it having any impact on our lives? Yet the Scriptures contain the mysteries of life and the means to joyful living! They are a primary avenue to encounter Christ who is the Way, the Truth, and the Life (cf. Jn 14:6).

The transformative power of the Scriptures has been proved in every generation: saints throughout the centuries have allowed the Bible to be the "two-edged sword" it proclaims itself to be. St. Anthony of the Desert abandoned his wealthy lifestyle in an instant after hearing the Gospel passage about the rich young man. St. Francis of Assisi wanted to make the Gospels the rule for his new order and spent his whole life conforming himself to the Jesus he found in those four books. These and many other saints were able to unlock the mystery of the Bible in such a way that it had life-changing implications. What is that mystery? *Every page of the Bible contains the potential for a life-changing encounter with Christ.*

How can we then unlock that mystery so that our own lives can be transformed? This book is intended to help you do just that.

In these pages I hope to lead you to a glimpse of the unbounded treasures of the Sacred Page, so that after glimpsing what it contains — whether for the first time or the thousandth — you will be able to more deeply explore the Scriptures for all their wonder and beauty. And there is no greater treasure to be found in the Bible than Jesus Christ himself. Christ is waiting to be discovered in the pages of the Bible, and it is of course in the Gospels where we meet him, as it were, face-to-face.

It is vitally important then to continually focus on the Gospels. The Church values these four documents more than any other writing, for only there can we find the words of Jesus himself. These incomparable and inspired writings reveal in a unique way aspects of the identity of Jesus, for, in addition to containing the very words of Christ, they offer the accounts of those who encountered him during his time on earth. They open a window into the realm of the person of Jesus, allowing us to see him as those who knew him did. Who did they think this man was? What were their hopes and dreams and fears regarding him? By examining Jesus through the eyes of his contemporaries, we can become more intimate with our Lord.

And yet the Gospels are not to be isolated from all the other sources of information about Christ, such as the writings of the Church Fathers, the lives of the saints, and the prayers of the Church. Each Gospel was written in the context of a believing and worshipping community founded by Christ himself, and was compiled with the purpose of demonstrating Christ's unique position in the plan of salvation. They were handed on from generation to generation, studied, and interpreted by saints and scholars in both East and West. But they are not simply dry texts insipidly studied by scholars; in every generation, men and women have been transformed by the inspired words they have found in the Gospels. By looking at centuries-old interpretations of these books — interpretations both written and lived — we are given fresh insights into their meaning. For these reasons, this book will make use of the entire tradition of the Church to dig deeper into the Sacred Word.

There are many ways to approach a study of Jesus in the Scriptures. Here, I take but one: an examination of the titles and names given to Jesus by those who knew him, as recorded in the Gospel of Matthew. In each chapter I study a single title or name, from the exalted ("Son of God") to the erroneous ("Ghost"), and reflect on how that appellation and the context in which it occurs deepen our understanding of the person of Jesus. Why does Jesus refer to himself as the "bridegroom"? What does it mean for us that the people of Nazareth dismiss him as a simple "carpenter's son"? What are the consequences of Christ being the "Lord of the Sabbath"? These and all the titles given to Jesus represent a single facet of the multidimensional person of the God-man. By restricting ourselves to the study of just one Gospel, we can explore that author's intentions in recording these specific titles. The evangelists had a myriad of names for Jesus they could have documented in their Gospels, but they chose the ones that would convey the overall picture of Christ they had in mind. Why does Matthew only record the title "Rabbi" on Judas' lips? What overall point did he want to communicate by his usage of the title "Son of God"?

As we examine each title and name given to Jesus in Matthew's Gospel, I pray that you will unlock some of the mysteries in the Gospel of Matthew and thereby encounter Christ in a new way, coming to a deeper appreciation of the beauty and grandeur that is our Savior.

And if you are wondering what happened to that young woman who read her Bible each day on the subway, she still loves to read the Scriptures. How do I know? A few years after that summer, I married her.

Man

"What sort of man is this?"

The book of Revelation bombards the reader with strange and mysterious sights, smells, and sounds. Creatures beyond man's imagination appear around every corner. In Chapter 4, John relates a vision of heaven in which "four living creatures" are grouped around the throne of God during the heavenly liturgy:

> And round the throne, on each side of the throne, are four living creatures, full of eyes in front and behind: the first living creature like a lion, the second living creature like an ox, the third living creature with the face of a man, and the fourth living creature like a flying eagle.
>
> And the four living creatures, each of them with six wings, are full of eyes all round and within, and day and night they never cease to sing, "Holy, holy, holy, is the Lord God Almighty, who was and is and is to come!"
>
> — Rev 4:6-8

These four creatures — who appear as a lion, an ox, a man, and an eagle — exist to direct praise to God, to direct the attention of all in heaven and earth toward the Almighty sitting on the eternal throne.

Throughout the centuries Christians have seen the various creatures and events in Revelation as symbols of people and events in salvation history. One of the most common interpretations of the four living creatures of Chapter 4 is that they represent the four Evangelists — Matthew, Mark, Luke, and John — who, with their Gospels, direct our minds and hearts to God Incarnate, Jesus Christ.

Among the variety of interpretations, the most common tradition originated with the great patristic Scripture scholar, St. Jerome. He sees Mark symbolized by the lion, which represents courage and strength — Mark begins his Gospel with the courageous John the Baptist calling all to repentance. Luke is represented by the ox because he begins his Gospel with Zechariah, the father of John the Baptist and a priest, whose responsibility is to offer animal sacrifice. The eagle represents John, whose prelude flies high above the earth and penetrates the mysteries of eternity deeply, like the eyes of an eagle. Finally, Matthew is represented by a man because his Gospel begins with Christ's human ancestry and the story of the Incarnation.

In conveying the Incarnation, Matthew delves into the greatest and most sublime of the Christian mysteries. How could God, the Almighty and Everlasting, become man? How could this man, Jesus of Nazareth, be God? Upon such a mystery man can contemplate and meditate, but he can never fully comprehend. Unfortunately, followers of Christ have at times misunderstood or twisted the relationship between God and man in Christ. Heresies have arisen in which the divinity of Christ was overemphasized to the neglect of his humanity; the reverse has been true in recent centuries.

Of course, in the time of Christ, there was no debate as to the reality of his humanity. It was as obvious as the sun rising in the east; here was a man like the rest of us. To the first-century Jew, the scandal — to understate the matter in the extreme — would have been the suggestion that Jesus might not have been only man, but also God Incarnate. The people who spent the most time with Jesus struggled deeply to penetrate this mystery. Nothing in their upbringing could prepare them for the possibility that the God of the universe would become man. In fact, their Jewish faith would be less likely than a pagan's to explain such an event. The God of the Jews was not just an extraordinary and powerful man, like many of the pagan gods. Instead, he was the One who created the universe out of nothing, holds it together by his will, and exists above all creation and time. For this God to become a limited, ordinary man was unthinkable.

The struggle to understand this mystery was especially evident in those who knew Christ best. The people of Nazareth knew Jesus as a babe at his mother's breast, a young boy playing with their children, and later as the local carpenter. Theories that Jesus was not mere man would gain no traction with them.

However, they didn't just struggle with the issue, they hardened their hearts to his divinity. Matthew recounts that when Jesus returned to his hometown, they exclaimed, "Where then did this man get all this?" (Mt 13:56) and they "took offense at him." They could not open their hearts to the possibility that one of their own could be extraordinary in some way. We can recognize how unsurprising this reaction is when we take an honest look at how critical we can be of those closest to us. It is easier by far to be open to the voice of God coming from faraway preachers or popular speakers than to hear the "still, small voice" of God that comes through everyday contact with family, friends, or coworkers. Daily contact can lead to a jaded heart, familiarity to closed ears.

But it is most often through these frequent interactions that the Lord speaks, teaching wisdom, patience, and humility. By being deaf to the voice of the Lord in our close relations, we deny God the ability to work through the mundane and the ordinary — thus denying the very basis of the Incarnation, as well as the sacraments. It is, in fact, more common for the Lord to send his graces through a spouse, a child, a coworker — or via water, bread, and wine — than through the exceptional or phenomenal. The people of Nazareth were expecting God to work through the exceptional, and that expectation made them blind to the most exceptional reality of all: that God had become, literally, one of them.

The Nazarenes were not the only ones to struggle with Christ's identity. His closest followers, the apostles, were not so hard of heart but were often left wondering how a man could do what Jesus did. Matthew recounts an instance of the apostles' confusion in the story of Jesus calming the storm. During this episode, while the storm is raging around them, Jesus is asleep — a simple detail that reveals both his humanity and his divinity. Like any man, he required sleep, but unlike other men, he did not fear the storm, knowing that his Father in Heaven would protect him. St. John Chrysostom says:

> How did they know he was a man? They could see him sleeping. He commanded a ship. So why were they so perplexed about his humanity, saying, "What sort of man is this?" His sleeping showed he was a man. His calming of the seas declared him God.
>
> — *Homily on the Gospel of Matthew* 28.1[1]

The apostles, however, many of whom were experienced seamen, do not share his serenity in the face of potential calamity. They wake him and beg his protection — already understanding in some way that he could do more to help them than just an ordinary man could. But after he calms the storm, they "marveled, saying, 'What sort of man is this, that even winds and sea obey him?'" (Mt 8:27). Matthew here is leading the reader to delve more deeply into the mystery of the Incarnation — he doesn't give an answer to the question he records because he wants the reader of his Gospel to ask himself the same thing: "What sort of man is this?"

These men who lived, slept, and ate with Jesus knew that he was truly a man. He hungered like the rest of them, got tired, and had all the limitations (save sin) they had. So they never questioned his humanity. They could not comprehend, however, how a simple man could do what Jesus did. Slowly, Jesus was bringing them to the realization that he was not only a man, but also God. Why didn't Jesus simply announce his divinity plainly to these, his closest followers? As a good teacher leads his students to discover truth for themselves — giving them, in this way, ownership of it — he led them to realize the mystery of his Godhood on their own. Through fits and starts, they do come to grasp it — and, eventually, give their lives for this truth.

Matthew himself is a great testament to this. Once a despised tax collector who most likely practiced his Jewish faith sporadically at best, he became a great evangelist, writing a Gospel, going to Ethiopia to preach the Good News, and shedding his blood there. Most surely when Christ first spoke to Matthew, the future apostle had no idea who it was that called him to leave his customs post — the eternal Son of God. Yet he responded nonetheless, with his small faith and limited knowledge. Over time, that faith and knowledge grew, transforming him into apostle, evangelist, and martyr.

The apostles spent three years living in close contact with Jesus. But another person was closer to Jesus than any other and never doubted that he was extraordinary, even divine: his mother, Mary. The mother who gave him birth, nursed him at her breast, and cared for him, of course, always knew he was truly man. But she, in her deep intimacy with Jesus, also knew he was God made flesh. Because she was completely open to God's revelation, pondering the mysteries of God in her heart (cf. Lk 2:19), she was able to see beyond the human level to the divine. This intimacy was possible through her daily interaction with Jesus. For the rest of us, Mary becomes the model for loving familiarity with Christ. Through prayer, that intimacy with the Lord and a deeper knowledge of the reality of his being reveals itself. Prayer is the key that unlocks the mysteries of Jesus Christ; as we contemplate more deeply the union between God and man in Christ, we are led to a deeper union between God and our own soul. Saints such as Teresa of Ávila, John of the Cross, and Thérèse of Lisieux show the rest of us the depths that this intimacy can reach through prayer.

Completely exposed to the workings of the Spirit, Mary says with confidence, "Do whatever he tells you" (Jn 2:5) and has absolute faith that it will be accomplished. Mary is the perfect disciple, becoming intimate with Jesus with an open heart so as to have his divine mysteries revealed to her. The deep connection between holiness and knowledge reveals itself in Mary. Being free from the stain of sin, Mary's mind is totally free to penetrate the divine mysteries, and she thus has an ability even the greatest theologian can never approach. To truly know the Lord — not just know *about* him but to *know* him — we must strive first and foremost to let grace clear our minds and bodies of their sinful burdens. Paraphrasing a maxim of the Christian East, "One cannot be a theologian who does not love God, and one who loves God is a theologian." Mary shows the path for understanding Christ — complete love for God and avoidance of sin.

The challenge for all Christians is to become more and more familiar with Jesus. In our walk with him, we can be like the people of Nazareth, or the apostles, or Mary. We can reject that Jesus is truly "extra-ordinary," surpassing the limitations placed on the possible; we can be like the apostles and struggle to make the human intellect grasp the mysterious ways of God; or, like Mary, we can become so intimate with Jesus, our brother in humanity, that we see him as who he is, God the Son who was made man for man's salvation. The Christian life for the most part is a movement from a Nazarene hard-heartedness to the struggling apostles' weak faith to Marian trust. And again, it is primarily prayer that opens the door from one state to the next. As a "Nazarene," we must pray for the grace to see beyond the natural to the supernatural. For a struggling apostle, prayer can lead to a deeper knowledge of the meaning of Christ's divinity. And finally, prayer can direct us to Marian trust, as we know that the impossible is possible for God.

Mary was a young Jewish girl who was told — by an angel, no less — the seemingly impossible: that she would virginally conceive a son. Not only a son, but the Son of God (cf. Lk 1:35). The vulnerability of her response, "Behold, I am the handmaid of the Lord; let it be to me according to your word" (Lk 1:38) shows how completely open she was to God's will in her life, no matter how improbable it seemed. The openness that Mary always possessed came more slowly to the apostles, but it did come. They eventually gave their lives in witness to the person of Jesus Christ. The model of the apostles allows the person of weak faith to see that God continues to work in each person to bring about a more complete acceptance of his will. Daily asking him for the grace to possess the required openness to believe that, for God, even the impossible is possible — such as God becoming man as a Jewish peasant — will lead to a more intimate, and more Marian, knowledge of him.

REFERENCES
Mt 8:27, 13:54

For Reflection
- How is God using those closest to me to speak to me?
- Do I let the little inconveniences of daily life be a means of spiritual growth?

Rabbi

"Hail, Rabbi!"

"Beware the Ides of March," said the soothsayer to Julius Caesar. And for good reason. On that very day in 44 B.C., after having declared himself dictator for life, Caesar would be assassinated by a group of senators led by his close friend, Marcus Brutus. This event, one of the classic acts of betrayal in western civilization, was immortalized by William Shakespeare in his play *Julius Caesar*. Upon recognizing Brutus as one of his assassins, Caesar famously says, "*Et tu, Brute?*" This laconic phrase has since entered the popular lexicon to denote any act of betrayal, and the "Ides of March," originally a festive day dedicated to the god Mars, has become synonymous with approaching doom.

Thus can a short word or phrase, through its association with a pivotal or shocking action, come to represent far more than its original and literal meaning. In Matthew's Gospel, the term "Rabbi" takes on just such a deeper, and tragic, meaning. Only twice is it used to refer to Jesus, but both times it is Judas Iscariot who uses the title. By placing this term solely on the lips of Christ's betrayer, Matthew transforms a first-century Jewish term of respect and admiration into perhaps the saddest word in all of his Gospel.

The first utterance occurs near the end of the Gospel, during the Last Supper. Christ has predicted that one of the Twelve will betray him. The apostles each ask, "Is it I, Lord?" while Judas asks, "Is it I, Rabbi?" (Mt 26:21-25; RSV translates "Rabbi" as "Master"). St. Jerome comments on this passage:

The others were grieved and very much saddened as they questioned Christ: "Surely, Lord, you don't mean me?" Lest he seem to betray himself by keeping silent, he [Judas] too, whose conscience was troubling him and who had boldly placed his hand in the dish, questioned him: "Surely, Rabbi, you don't mean me?" To this he added lip homage and a show of incredulity. The others, who were not traitors, said, "Surely, Lord, you don't mean us?" He who was the traitor did not call him Lord but Rabbi, as if to have an excuse, upon rejecting the Lord, for having betrayed at most a Rabbi. Jesus answered, "You have said so." The traitor was put to shame by the same response Christ would later give to Pilate.

— Commentary on Matthew 4.26.25 [2]

The other instance of Judas calling Jesus "Rabbi" occurs just a few hours later. He approaches Christ in the Garden of Gethsemane and announces for all to hear, "Hail, Rabbi!", before giving the signal of betrayal to the chief priests and elders by kissing Jesus. In response, Christ — with echoes of *"Et tu, Brute?"*— answers, "Friend, why are you here?" (Mt 26:47-50).

The only other use of the term "Rabbi" in Matthew's Gospel (Mt 23:7-8) shows that it is not a term to be employed under the new economy instituted by Christ:

> "You are not to be called rabbi, for you have one teacher, and you are all brethren."

— Mt 23:8

Why does Matthew give the term "Rabbi" such negative connotations? Such is not the case with the other Gospel writers: Mark and John use this title in positive or neutral ways; Luke, being a Gentile, never uses this Hebrew word in his Gospel. Since Matthew was writing to a specifically Jewish Christian audience, we might expect that this peculiarly Jewish title would be used more positively. Yet by placing it in the mouth of Judas, Matthew emphasizes his primary theme: that Jesus is inaugurating a new covenant that fulfills and supersedes the old, and thus the old ways of relating to God and his representatives are no longer valid. Jesus is no simple Rabbi; as the other eleven apostles proclaim at the Last Supper, he is "Lord."

But to a first-century Jew like Judas, "Rabbi" was still a term of great respect. His application of this title to Christ highlights the depths of his betrayal. It is quite astounding — shocking, even — to this day. By hailing Jesus, he betrays him. Greeting him with a term of admiration, he hands Jesus over like a common thief to be killed with thieves. This story is so familiar that it is easy to lose sight of the depth of its sadness. For anyone to be let down by a friend is difficult enough, but for Jesus to be betrayed in so callous a fashion by one to whom he had given almost three years of his life had to be breathtakingly painful. Jesus surrounded himself with many friends, family, and associates. He truly depended upon them for the success of his mission — they were not "extras" in the plan of salvation. But by being dependent upon others, he opened himself up to the possibility of betrayal. Thus, Jesus joins humanity in the anguish that inevitably comes with human relationships. In making himself vulnerable to men and women, Christ joins humanity in experiencing the pain and hurt that are too often part and parcel of friendship, marriage, and family. His betrayal becomes one of the sufferings that Christ brings to the cross. And by overcoming it in his death and resurrection — and even using it as a pivotal means to bring about the redemption of mankind — Christ gives Christians the ability to unite their own experiences of betrayal with his on the cross. By doing so, he does not remove the pain that betrayal brings, but shares in it and uses it for the salvation of others.

How does Christ respond when Judas denies that he will betray Christ? Jesus offers Judas, along with the other apostles, his very body and blood in the Eucharist (Mt 26:26-28). Instead of rejecting Judas or holding back from him, Jesus invites him into the mystical communion possible only through the Eucharist. Even at this late hour, he gives Judas the opportunity to repent and return to communion with Christ — indeed, to partake more fully in the mystery of his love. Christ's every action at the Last Supper shows that he yearns to bring Judas to repentance, up to the very moment of his betrayal. As St. John Chrysostom relates:

> Even before the supper he had washed the feet of Judas. See how he spares the traitor. He did not say, "Judas, you will betray me," but only "one of you will betray me." This was again to offer time for repentance by keeping his identity concealed. He was willing to allow all the others to be alarmed, just for the sake of redeeming this one.
>
> — *Homily on the Gospel of Matthew* 81.1[3]

Jesus treats every person in this way: even though all of us betray him through each sin that we commit, he still offers himself to each of us, constantly giving himself in order to bring us back into communion with him. He never holds back, never refuses to pour out his life for the reconciliation of sinners.

Why *did* Judas betray Christ? Over the centuries, many have speculated on the notions behind Judas' betrayal — how to explain the inexplicable act of betraying him through whom all things were created? Traditional thought has run along the lines of base motives such as greed, an interpretation founded on the apostle John's perspective. John has little sympathy for Judas, calling him a thief (Jn 12:6), and telling us that Judas had allowed Satan to enter into him (Jn 12:27). But in modern times it has become more fashionable to try to mitigate the enormity of Judas' betrayal. Some have even conjectured that Judas was trying to force Christ's hand, believing that his arrest would hasten the coming of the Messianic Age. If this was the case, Judas was ironically correct, although he woefully misunderstood how that Age would be inaugurated.

Whatever the reason for the betrayal, it is clear that Judas, in spite of spending day and night with Jesus for years, did not understand him or his mission. By calling him *Rabbi*, he demonstrates that he still views Jesus as part of the only system he knows: the nationalistic Jewish ideal founded on King David. He cannot perceive that Jesus has come to fulfill, and thus replace, the entire Jewish way of life with a new covenant that will go beyond a simple nation-state. Judas came to Jesus' service not in humility and a spirit of learning, but with the hope that Jesus could further his own goals. Judas does not acknowledge Jesus as Lord and submit to his agenda; he wants Jesus to be the instrument of his own personal plans. This is a temptation that all Christians face: instead of being passive to the dominion of Christ, we expect him to further our own desires and projects.

Judas wanted personal salvation on his own terms, not on God's. He who betrayed Jesus in a garden conformed himself to Satan — who, in the original Garden, refused to give dominion to God. In both instances, the result is death, but God, in his wonderful mercy, uses the sin in the Garden of Gethsemane to undo the sin in the Garden of Eden. He overcomes Satan's betrayal of man through Judas' betrayal of himself. Here, then, is the power of love: it can defeat even the most harmful betrayal and hurt. Openness to love helps a Christian resist the pull of bitterness that betrayal brings. Bitterness offers only a mirage of satisfaction, while in reality it magnifies the pain. Love, though, even in the face of betrayal, overcomes pain and redeems it.

The world has never understood this and will never understand it. The Old Testament law of justice "an eye for an eye, and a tooth for a tooth" (Ex 21:24) was a comparatively compassionate, not vindictive, idea of justice in the ancient world. The pagan societies that surrounded Israel, unenlightened by divine revelation, applied the ultimate retaliation for the simplest offense; the pagan law of justice was "a life for an eye, a life for a tooth." God in his loving condescension was patiently leading his people to a higher law — one based on love, one that rejected such views of revenge. Jesus brings this concept to its fullness: love your enemies; turn the other cheek. When attacked or betrayed, the believer must not respond in kind — not only for the sake of the attacker but for his own sake as well. Revenge, being an offspring of the devil, is sterile, but love, being the very life of God, is fertile and life-giving.

In hindsight, it's all too easy to condemn Judas for his refusal to submit to God's plans through Christ. But the "logic" of Judas is not uncommon in the thinking of Christians even today: desiring to control our life, or limit what God can do in it, is following in the footsteps of Judas. The temptation can manifest itself in a refusal to believe that God can overcome a serious, persistent sin, or in a rejection of suffering as a means to deeper union with God. Intimacy with Christ is no guarantee of protection from such thinking: Judas was with Jesus for three years, communing with him daily, and did good works in his name. But Christ never forces himself on another, even those closest to him. He always — daily — invites us to communion with him. Throughout Christ's ministry, Judas' heart had remained set on his own desires and dreams. It had become hardened, unable to be open to the grace of Christ. The same can happen in the life of the most pious of Christians: convinced that our desires and plans must be God's desires and plans, we refuse to submit to the Lord in all things. But a disciple must humbly conform himself in all ways to Christ, as beautifully expressed in the communion prayer of the *Divine Liturgy of St. John Chrysostom*:

> Of your mystical supper, O Son of God, accept me today as a communicant; for I will not speak of your mystery to your enemies; neither like Judas will I give you a kiss; but like the thief will I confess you: remember me, O Lord in your kingdom.

The Lord — who, even to the end, tried to bring Judas to repentance — will respond in love to such a supplication, leading us to a deeper union with him, a union Judas foolishly rejected.

REFERENCES

Mt 26:25, 26:49

For Reflection

- Do I want salvation on my own terms?
- Are there parts of my life I refuse to let God change? Betrayals in my life I refuse to forgive?

Ghost

They were terrified, saying, "It is a ghost!"

"Be not afraid!" Pope John Paul II thundered to the world, upon his introduction as the 263rd successor of St. Peter. This was in recognition of and a direct attack upon the debilitating effects of fear of all kinds, especially its effects on the spiritual life. His was a voice in the twentieth-century wilderness, a world engulfed in fear and living under the threat of nuclear annihilation. Yet he called the human race to be unafraid. This was not a call based on naiveté or Pollyanna-style optimism. John Paul had seen human evil at its worst under both Nazi and Communist regimes. He recognized the dehumanizing effects of some economic and governmental systems. He knew well the terrifying evil of which man is capable. He still called, even demanded, that Christians not be afraid.

John Paul's strength in the face of evil was not based on human courage, but upon trust. Only because he put complete trust in the providence and love of God could he lead the charge against fear, desiring that all Christians would follow. The man of faith must, by definition, trust in God and abandon himself to God's providence and love; this is true courage. Without an utter dependence upon God, he will not believe in what he cannot see; he will assume the worst and be controlled by his fears. He must understand that his own powers cannot protect him, but that God, in his loving mercy, will.

Fear is perhaps the most dominant emotion driving man to action — or, often enough, freezing him in inaction. It can prevent tasks as benign as a trip to the dentist or as serious as doing one's duty on the battlefield. Fear grips the soul and quickens the heart. We magnify the potential danger as our mind dwells on it, causing greater and greater paralysis. Fear directly assaults one of the cardinal virtues and essential requirements of being a disciple: fortitude, the virtue that gives one the strength to do good and avoid evil, regardless of the consequences.

Jesus' closest comrades were not immune to fear, as more than one biblical passage shows us. Matthew 14:22-33, for instance, describes a scene dominated by this primordial emotion. It begins benignly enough, with Jesus sending his apostles ahead of him on the boat after the miraculous feeding of the five thousand. Their master has just demonstrated in front of thousands great power that not only satisfies the crowds, but also hearkens back to the manna God fed the Israelites in the desert. Many of their hopes and dreams regarding a coming Messianic Age appear to be unfolding before their very eyes, in the person of Jesus. What a spiritual high they must be experiencing as they step onto the boat, assured of their own places in the kingdom about to unfold.

Reality comes crashing into their dreams in the form of a fierce storm. Matthew recounts that the boat was "beaten by the waves" (Mt 14:24). A thought must have crept into their minds — surely this is not how it would end? After seeing Jesus apparently coming into his glory, were they going to simply be lost at sea, never to be seen again? Without the presence of Jesus in their midst, they have put their trust in human strength and find it lacking.

Then, as if things aren't already anxious enough, a figure appears, walking toward them *on the water!* What was before a frightful occurrence of nature has suddenly been overshadowed by a terrifying supernatural encounter. The apostles' nerves are so frayed now that their reaction is entirely predictable: "They were terrified" (Mt 14:26). As their fears increase exponentially, they proclaim, "It is a ghost!" (Mt 14:26) — perhaps there to lead them to the afterlife that appears to be in their immediate future.

But then, a familiar voice rings out, bringing them from terror to elation. "Take heart, it is I: *have no fear*" (Mt 14:27, emphasis added). The original Greek, translated "it is I" in the RSV, is *ego eimi* — literally, "I AM," the same phrase used by God to identify himself to Moses at the burning bush (Ex 3:14). Christ does not tell them not to be afraid because he will save them, or that he will remove the storm; they are to be unafraid simply because they are in his divine presence. He is the only one who can truly banish their fears. Only he can, by his very existence, make fear take flight. Here is the balm for all the apostles' anxieties: the person of Jesus. Knowing that he is with them casts aside those anxieties, for they know that he will protect and guide them.

Peter readily — impetuously, even— trusts in Jesus; he is the one able to overcome his fear and, consistent with his impulsive nature, move into action. He calls out, "Lord, if it is you, bid me come to you on the water" (Mt 14:28). Peter wants to step out in faith — literally. He doesn't want to wait for Jesus to enter the boat; he wants to depend totally and miraculously on Jesus to protect him. He walks out onto the water. And Jesus does protect him, keeping him safe from sinking. However, "when [Peter] saw the wind, *he was afraid*, and beginning to sink he cried out, 'Lord, save me'" (Mt 14:30, emphasis added). Peter is unable to conquer his fear completely by throwing himself totally in Christ's hands. Following rapidly on the heels of his initial trust comes fear again, when he sees the danger of the wind. Although he trusted Jesus to give him the ability to do the impossible by walking on water, there is a limit to his faith. When that faith comes under attack, he no longer trusts in God's power completely, and he begins to sink.

Christ said that even small faith is able to move mountains (Mt 21:21), yet fear puts faith to flight, diminishing its power and strength. Peter shows us that even faith that allows for the miraculous can dissipate in the face of immediate danger. Yet even in his weakness, he still cries out to Christ, "Save me" (Mt 14:30) — something must remain of his faith — and Christ rescues him from danger.

This episode prefigures Peter's future threefold denial. The apostle boldly steps out onto the water, just as he would later proclaim boldly that he would never deny Christ. But when trials come, he falters — here, due to the wind; later, due to the danger of being arrested with Jesus. Yet ultimately, he cries out to Jesus for salvation, and Christ lovingly restores him. In both cases, Peter must first learn of his own weakness before he can truly cry out to Jesus in faith and utter dependence.

The storm at sea occurs during the dark of night, enhancing the fearful atmosphere that pervades the scene. In Sunday Night Prayer, the Church professes, "Night holds no terrors for me sleeping under God's wings," using these words as the antiphon for Psalm 91. A meditation on the human emotion of fear, this psalm beautifully captures the faithful person's trust in God in spite of the fearful realities of the world. Both the psalm (in v. 5) and the antiphon introducing it recognize the truth that darkness brings about fear. Physical darkness can indeed reveal the fear of what threatens the body, as the apostles experienced in the storm. Its cousin, spiritual darkness, however, afflicts the soul at its deepest level. Fundamentally, all instances of spiritual darkness derive from the soul's perception that God is absent. The Lord has created each person with an elemental dependence upon him. When a soul fails to recognize this dependence, emptiness ensues, accompanied perhaps by spiritual dryness, feelings of abandonment, or even depression. Peter's final cry to Jesus shows us that the antidote for such feelings is trust: trust that God is truly present, in spite of all apparent evidence to the contrary. Such trust, however, is not a feeling; it is an act of the will. The prayer of St. Faustina, "Jesus,

I trust in You," is tailor-made not for the times we are resting in Christ's bosom, but for when we are most unsure of his presence.

Trusting someone forges an attachment — an attachment based on dependence. Psalm 91 tells us upon whom we are to place our trust:

> He who dwells in the shelter of the Most High,
>   who abides in the shadow of the Almighty,
> will say to the LORD, "My refuge and my fortress;
> my God, in whom I trust."
> For he will deliver you from the snare of the fowler
>   and from the deadly pestilence;
> he will cover you with his pinions,
>   and under his wings you will find refuge;
>   his faithfulness is a shield and buckler.
> You will not fear the terror of the night,
>   nor the arrow that flies by day,
> nor the pestilence that stalks in darkness,
>   nor the destruction that wastes at noonday.
>
> — Ps 91:1-6

Dependence like this can be a fearful thing; trust means vulnerability. Rejection and betrayal are lurking possibilities, and our hearts urge us to erect barriers that feel like insurance against vulnerability. But the resulting self-reliance is contrary to Gospel living, in which the believer works toward total dependence on God. Jesus urges his followers to this complete dependence upon our heavenly Father:

> "Therefore I tell you, do not be anxious about your life, what you shall eat or what you shall drink, nor about your body, what you shall put on . . . [S]eek first his kingdom and his righteousness, and all these things shall be yours as well.
>
> "Therefore do not be anxious about tomorrow, for tomorrow will be anxious for itself. Let the day's own trouble be sufficient for the day."
>
> — Mt 6:25, 33-34

Life brings struggles that are difficult, even seemingly impossible, to bear. Whether it be the death of a loved one, the despair born from a persistent sin, or perhaps the daily stress of the modern world, life is scary. We may suspect that even God is not powerful enough to overcome such things. But Christ comes into our lives and cries out: "Take heart, it is I: *have no fear*" (Mt 14:27). It is Christ who will dispel the fears of this world and lead his followers to courageous trust in the Father. The Christian response to fear is not to run from it or to be overrun by it, but to step out of the boat and grab onto Jesus, trusting in his providence and love, and trusting that Christ will never let go. Living as we do with our imperfect natures it is easy to slip and fall, but we look to Peter as our model — even when he fell, he still cried out to Christ, to whom else would he go? (cf. Jn 6:68).

Pope John Paul II could boldly proclaim "Be Not Afraid!" because he knew the promise of Christ: "I AM, have no fear" (Mt 14:27). Christ is no ghost, but the solid rock, the refuge, and fortress that will withstand the storms of life. We can trust in Christ with confidence and say with St. Paul:

> For I am sure that neither death, nor life, nor angels, nor principalities, nor things present, nor things to come, nor powers, nor height, nor depth, nor anything else in all creation, will be able to separate us from the love of God in Christ Jesus our Lord.
>
> — Rom 8:38-39

REFERENCES
Mt 14:26

For Reflection
- How do I let fear control my life?
- Is fear keeping me from completely surrendering my life to Christ?
- How does it hold me back?

Carpenter's Son

"Is not this the carpenter's son?"

As all who have experienced it will testify, the wonders of a new love seize the soul and flood the heart. All thoughts are of the beloved and all actions are directed toward her. A burning desire grows within you to learn everything possible about the one loved. No detail is unworthy of notice when related to her loveliness. The unspoken supposition underlying this hunger is that the more you know about a loved one, the more you have to love about her.

This is true as well of the Christian's love for Jesus Christ: intense love will instill in a Christian the desire to know more and more about the man from Galilee, launching a quest to uncover every possible detail about this life-changing person.

However, Christians through the centuries have been largely frustrated in one aspect of this search for knowledge: the dearth of information about the private earthly life of Jesus. Given that he is the central figure of the Christian faith, his life is amazingly obscure. Matthew skips from the remarkable events surrounding Christ's birth to the preaching of John the Baptist thirty years later — seeing no reason, apparently, to pass on in written form any of the particulars of Jesus' childhood, adolescence, or early adulthood. What was his personality as a child? When did Joseph die? How did that affect him? What kind of student was he at the local synagogue? These questions and others like them, which have tickled the ears of Christians hungry for any detail about their Lord, will ultimately go unanswered on this side of eternity.

Not that followers of Jesus haven't tried to fill in the gaps of his human life. Originating around the fourth century and continuing until Renaissance times, legends circulated of Jesus performing many miracles as a boy, typically precocious in nature. From fashioning live birds out of clay to toppling pagan temples with just a thought, Jesus would seem to have had an active childhood. One can just imagine Mary and Joseph exchanging knowing and possibly exasperated glances on such occasions. Had these sorts of things actually happened, they surely would have impressed his fellow Nazarenes. Yet, based on the townspeople's reaction to his public ministry when he returned to Nazareth to preach, the veracity of such stories is questionable.

> And when Jesus had finished these parables, he went away from there, and coming to his own country he taught them in their synagogue, so that they were astonished, and said, "Where did this man get this wisdom and these mighty works? Is not this the carpenter's son? Is not his mother called Mary? And are not his brothers James and Joseph and Simon and Judas? And are not all his sisters with us? Where then did this man get all this?"
> — Mt 13:53-56

If Jesus had been performing wonders as a child, think about the anticipation that would have followed his return to Nazareth from preaching in the neighboring towns of Galilee. Once he comes home, however, this text seems to show the opposite: Jesus' fellow Nazarenes are completely dumbfounded as to the origin of his apparently newfound knowledge. These neighbors would have seen Jesus day in and day out for thirty years; they knew he had no special rabbinical training, no philosophical background, no connection to Jewish mystical communities. Their own sons would have taken classes at the synagogue with him under the same teachers. They would have interacted with him in their places of business, discussing the issues of the day. Most likely, they would have perceived Jesus as a thoughtful, if quiet, man, prone to think of others in the most charitable light, yet given to anger against those that mock God —

but as a sage or mystic? Unlikely. The wisdom that Christ possessed had lain dormant, not revealing itself to his neighbors until his "hour" had come. Wisdom is generally understood to be a gift acquired over a lifetime; the Nazarenes could not understand how Jesus could acquire his wisdom so quickly and so suddenly.

And where *did* he get this wisdom? The answer would have startled even the most accepting Nazarene: Jesus *is* the Wisdom Incarnate of the Father. St. Paul proclaims, "Christ [is] . . . the wisdom of God" (1 Cor 1:24) and "God made [Christ Jesus] our wisdom" (1 Cor 1:30). The Church Fathers delighted in recognizing Christ as the speaker in the soliloquy of personified Wisdom, found in Proverbs 8:22-31:

> The LORD created me at the beginning of his work,
>> the first of his acts of old.
> Ages ago I was set up,
>> at the first, before the beginning of the earth.
> When there were no depths I was brought forth,
>> when there were no springs abounding with water.
> Before the mountains had been shaped,
>> before the hills, I was brought forth;
> before he had made the earth with its fields,
>> or the first of the dust of the world.
> When he established the heavens,
>> I was there,
> when he drew a circle on the face of the deep,
> when he made firm the skies above,
>> when he established the fountains of the deep,
> when he assigned to the sea its limit,
>> so that the waters might not transgress his command,
> when he marked out the foundations of the earth,
>> then I was beside him, like a master workman;
> and I was daily his delight, rejoicing before him always,
>> rejoicing in his inhabited world
>> and delighting in the sons of men.

Jesus does not only obtain wisdom in his humanity; he is Wisdom personified in his divinity. The question on the lips of the people of Nazareth — "Where did this man get this wisdom?" — reveals the reason for their inability to answer their own question: they only considered Jesus a "man," and it seemed impossible for a simple man, a carpenter's son, to have such wisdom with only the modest education and life experiences of a Nazarene. Christ allowed the source of his wisdom to remain a mystery to them, keeping it hidden until his public ministry had begun.

Thus, the people of Nazareth were "astonished" by the wisdom of Christ, a clear indicator that Jesus had done little to distinguish himself over the years. Most likely, Jesus chose to grow up in a fashion no different than the other Nazarene boys. And this is how Jesus' townsfolk perceived him, asking, "Is not this the carpenter's son?" (Mt 13:55): their primary conception of Jesus centered around his family, and, by extension, his livelihood — a son typically did the same work as his father. His neighbors identified in him no special insights into God or the religious world; he was just an ordinary man. Although St. Paul proclaims that "in him all things were created, in heaven and on earth, visible and invisible" (Col 1:16), the people of Nazareth appeared to be more familiar with his ability to create their plows and shelves.

From this, one may deduce that Jesus must have embraced the life of an ordinary man completely. He did not consider the everyday aspects of human existence — family and work — something to be ignored or glossed over in favor of theological exhortations and mystical experiences. When God became man, he truly meant it: he was truly the son of a carpenter. As the perfect Son of God, the life of Jesus was to do the will of the Father; thus, his ordinary life, preceding his public ministry, must have had a purpose in the Divine Plan as well. Why, then, did he humble himself, becoming not just "man" but a common, ordinary man?

St. Paul points to the answer in his Letter to the Romans. He writes:

> For if while we were enemies we were reconciled to God by the
> death of his Son, much more, now that we are reconciled, shall
> we be saved by his life. . . . For as by one man's disobedience
> many were made sinners, so by one man's obedience many will
> be made righteous.
>
> — Rom 5:10, 19

Christ's mission was to undo the work of Adam. The disobedience of the first man — Adam — brought disorder and death into the world; the obedience of the second Adam — Jesus — would bring restoration and redemption to the world. Adam's actions brought about the Fall through disobedience, but Christ would bring about restoration by his *whole life* of obedience. Although the climax of this obedience was the cross, it had its origin in Bethlehem and continued in Nazareth.

Christ's mission of restoration was directed first and foremost at the union between God and man that was ruptured in Eden, a union restored only by his obedient death and resurrection. That disunion was not the only consequence of the Fall, however; our first parents' action also ruptured the *earthly* life of man, especially its two integral aspects: human relationships and human labor.

This rupture is clear from the Genesis account of the Fall. After Adam and Eve sinned against God by eating the fruit of the tree of knowledge of good and evil, Genesis recounts:

> Then the eyes of both were opened, and they knew that they
> were naked; and they sewed fig leaves together and made
> themselves aprons.
>
> — Gen 3:7

Before the Fall, Adam and Eve had been in perfect harmony with each other. They were able to be vulnerable with one another, trusting completely in the other. This is how all human relationships were intended to be. However, the Fall brought discord to this harmony, a discord that was humanly impossible to repair. Now men and women would no longer trust each other completely, and would seek protection in order to prevent pain and hurt from others. History is a testament to failed relationships: from the discord in families to the conflict between nations, the human race is unable to live in peace. It seems that an underlying distrust defines human relationships, as each person is concerned primarily with self, rather than with serving the other. The exaltation of self that was Adam's sin is the origin of this human discord.

Along with human dissension, another fruit of the Fall is the disordering of labor. Prior to the incident with the serpent, God commanded man to "till and keep" the Garden (Gen 2:15); work, in other words, is not the effect of sin, it precedes the Fall and is part of paradise. But this original work was one of harmony with the earth. God had placed the animals and plants of the earth under the dominion of man to serve him (cf. Gen 1:26-29) — thus work was not intended to be laborious and difficult and necessary for survival, but a means of deepening man's relationship with creation. After the Fall, however, God declares:

"Because you have listened to the voice of your wife,
        and have eaten of the tree
of which I commanded you,
        'You shall not eat of it,'
cursed is the ground because of you;
        in toil you shall eat of it all the days of your life;
thorns and thistles it shall bring forth to you;
        and you shall eat the plants of the field.
In the sweat of your face
        you shall eat bread
till you return to the ground,
        for out of it you were taken;
you are dust,
        and to dust you shall return."

— Gen 3:17-19

Now, work would be a battle between man and nature: instead of creation serving man and supplying his material needs, man would need to labor heavily just to survive.

Throughout history, man has struggled to subdue nature. Christ's life was not exempt from this law. As a carpenter, he had to struggle and sweat and labor to form the wood into the shapes and designs he desired. When he made a mistake, he had to start over. When he had an accident, the pain was no less than any carpenter's. While in today's world immense effort has been expended on technology with the goal of reducing the burden of labor upon man, this effort has not truly removed its yoke. Although survival is no longer an issue for most of us, the technology-dependent society we have fashioned moves at a frenetic pace that disrupts the life of prayer and the ability to commune with God and others. Work — intended originally as a means of uniting humanity to creation, and thus, the Creator — has instead become a barrier to communion with God and his handiwork.

In light of these two consequences of the Fall, the value of Christ's "hidden" life becomes apparent. It was not simply a time for Jesus to wait until his public ministry — his "real work" — could begin. It was a carpenter's son who won for mankind its salvation: he was a true member of a specific human family, and a true artisan in his craft. Every moment of his life, from doing chores for his mother to following the directions of his earthly father, was offered to the Heavenly Father for humanity's sake. Through this "hidden" life, Christ's work of redemption encompasses everything harmed by Adam's sin, both spiritual and earthly.

Thus, work and human relationships are the arenas in which the imitation of Christ takes place. The mundane tasks of life must not be looked upon as obstacles to holiness but as the path to it. By quietly accepting the ordinary responsibilities in life, we join our actions to Christ's redeeming life and participate in reversing the curse of Adam and Eve. In his letter to the Colossians, St. Paul details the means of achieving this harmonious life:

> And *whatever you do, in word or deed, do everything in the name of the Lord Jesus,* giving thanks to God the Father through him.
>
> Wives, be subject to your husbands, as is fitting in the Lord. Husbands, love your wives, and do not be harsh with them. Children, obey your parents in everything, for this pleases the Lord. Fathers, do not provoke your children, lest they become discouraged. . . . Whatever your task, work heartily, as serving the Lord and not men, knowing that from the Lord you will receive the inheritance as your reward; you are serving the Lord Christ.
>
> — Col 3:17-21, 23-24 (emphasis added)

So it is by joining our actions to Christ that they are made redemptive.

On the cross, Jesus offered his thirty-three years of human existence to the Father — not only his preaching, teaching, healings, and suffering, but also the common experiences of human relationships and labor that were bound for obscurity. No human action, therefore, is obscured from the sight of the Father, who accepts all works united to the work of his Son, regardless of their apparent impact on earth. Through Christ's embrace of the toil of human life, from the toil of building human relationships to the toil of labor, he elevates that life to a means of salvation.

REFERENCES
Mt 13:55

For Reflection
- Do I see the routine aspects of my daily life as a means to holiness?
- Do I embrace my work, whether as a housewife, a priest, or a businessman, as a means to draw closer to Christ?

John the Baptist

"Who do men say that the Son of man is?"
And they said, "Some say John the Baptist . . ."

First-century Palestine. The Jewish religion, that most ancient and noble of faiths, has become calcified and stale. The religious leaders are consumed with infighting, busy imposing petty rules that burden the faithful. Oppression by foreign powers, now a way of life, adds to the burden and makes the dream of a Davidic kingdom seem distant and remote. It has been centuries since God sent a prophet; had God finally abandoned his chosen people after all of their rejections of his covenant?

> . . . there is no longer any prophet,
>   and there is none among us who knows how long.
> How long, O God, is the foe to scoff?
>   Is the enemy to revile thy name for ever?
>
> — Ps 74:9-10

Into this dismal scene erupts a magnificent fire, lighting the hearts of men and women throughout the land: "Have you heard about John, the son of Zechariah?" "Come down to the Jordan to listen to him and be baptized." "He might be the Messiah!"

Finally God had sent a prophet — perhaps more than a prophet — to turn the nation of Israel back to him and restore its withered glory. Everyone was talking about this preacher of repentance, hoping against hope that maybe he would be the one — the one to deliver Israel and start the new Messianic Age promised so long ago.

Then another figure appears, enigmatic and unlike any previous prophet. First, he seems to be a disciple of John, being baptized by him and preaching the same message of repentance. But this man from Nazareth is different. John is deferential to him, not the other way around. Instead of pointing to another who is to come, he points to himself. John's followers begin to leave him for this new preacher named Jesus. Then, John is arrested for obstinately confronting Herod about the tetrarch's irregular marriage, and he is beheaded. Once word reaches the people about his death, they know that John cannot be the Messiah; the Messiah, they were sure, would never be so shamefully executed.

People begin to look now to Jesus, wondering if he will avoid the fate of the Baptist. Some even believe him to *be* John. When Jesus asked his disciples, "Who do men say that the son of man is?" they answered, "Some say John the Baptist" (Mt 16:14). Clearly, many in the crowds recognized the similarity of their messages and thought that the messenger was one and the same, concluding that the tale of John's beheading was just an inaccurate rumor. But Herod, who had killed John, also believed Jesus to be the Baptist, though by way of altogether different reasoning: he believed that John, who continued to haunt his dreams at night, had returned from the dead to keep challenging his immoral lifestyle.

This fusion of identity between John and Jesus is noteworthy. Though John had neither risen from the dead nor changed his name to Jesus, the power that moved him also moved Jesus; there was a deep unity of purpose between the two. John himself, of course, would have quickly disabused anyone of the notion that he and Jesus should even be spoken of in the same breath. It was clear to him the gulf that lay between his cousin and himself: "He who is coming after me is mightier than I, whose sandals I am not worthy to carry" (Mt 3:11). John's purpose in life was the same as the purpose of the whole of the Old Testament — to prepare the people for the coming of the Christ. Jesus said that "all the prophets and the law prophesied until John" (Mt 11:13); all of the work of the Old Covenant was leading to the one who would then point to Jesus and say, "Behold, the Lamb of God, who takes away the sin of the world!" (Jn 1:29). The Baptist recognized that his role was that of a sign pointing to the deeper reality; he was a messenger proclaiming tidings of another. John *preached* the Word of God; Jesus *was* the Word of God. Origen, the first great Scripture scholar of the Church, uses the illuminating imagery of the connection between voice and speech to express the unity between John and Jesus:

> [A]s the Saviour is speech, John is voice. John himself invites me to take this view of him, for to those who asked who he was, he answered, "I am the voice of one crying in the wilderness, Prepare the way of the Lord! make His paths straight!" . . . A voice must be perceived with the ears if the mind is afterwards to receive the speech which the voice indicates. Hence, John is, in point of his birth, a little older than Christ, for our voice comes to us before our speech. But John also points to Christ; for speech is brought forward by the voice. . . . In a word, when John points out Christ, it is man pointing out God, the Saviour incorporeal, the voice pointing out the Word.
>
> — *Commentary on John* 26 [4]

Just as one cannot have speech without a voice, John's mission was a necessary part of salvation history; without the voice of the Baptist, the way would not have been prepared for the Word who was to fill up the world. Everything about John points to Jesus; as Origen asserts, "Speech is brought forward by the voice." Thus, the mission of Christ is brought forth by the preparation of John.

John's role in salvation history required deep humility on his part. His whole inner being was directed toward the glorification of another and the diminishment of himself. "He must increase, but I must decrease" (Jn 3:30). This could not have been an easy task for John. He lived in an age that yearned for a prophetic leader, and he was a perfect fit, hearkening to the days of Nathan or Elijah. It would not have been difficult to mold his message ever so subtly to increase his own stature, yet he refused to do so. St. Gregory the Great explains:

> Because people had seen that John the Baptist was endowed with astonishing holiness, they believed . . . that he was the Christ, as is said in the Gospel. The people were deliberating, all questioning in their hearts concerning John, whether perhaps he might be the Christ, and they asked him, "Are you the Christ?" If John had not been a valley in his own eyes, he would not have been full of the grace of the Spirit.
>
> — *Forty Gospel Homilies* 6[5]

John's humility made him see himself as "a valley in his own eyes." Humility, an honest assessment of one's status before God, is the fundamental characteristic of a saint, for a saint's primary role is the same as John's: to point to the Lord. The path of holiness is one in which a person decreases, so that Christ might increase within. This became so true for St. Paul that he could write, "It is no longer I who live, but Christ who lives in me" (Gal 2:20). John the Baptist, by emptying himself of his own pride, became a conduit, fulfilling the prophecy of Malachi: "I send my messenger to prepare the way before me" (Mal 3:1). Each Christian is called to fulfill this prophecy as well, preparing the souls of others for the coming of the Lord.

Many of us, however, do not think of humility when we think of John the Baptist. We picture John as a half-crazed, self-righteous zealot, lacking in love and compassion. Jesus meanwhile has come to be seen as simply a caring and tolerant guide. Obviously, this is a misconception from both angles. John, in calling all people to repentance, was full of love and compassion. It was because he understood very clearly the damage sin does that he so desired that each person would turn to God for forgiveness and peace. He trusted completely in the mercy of God — that he would forgive any who came to him in humility and sincerity. The baptism John offered was the very practice of mercy; it was a sign reminding people of the forgiveness of a merciful God for those who repent. John's whole mission, therefore, was filled with the love of God. Even his very condemnation of Herod's sham marriage to his sister-in-law was an act of love. He knew that Herod's sin not only harmed Herod but, by its public nature, harmed others through the scandal it caused. He, like his master, was willing to give up his life in love for others. He knew that if he ignored such a public disregard for the institution of marriage, he would be allowing destructive forces to be unleashed against all families. John thus became a martyr for the sanctity of marriage.

Jesus' preaching was of one accord with John's. His first proclamation is simply a continuation of John's ministry: "Repent, for the kingdom of heaven is at hand" (Mt 4:17). And like John, he recognized the importance of marriage in human relations. In fact, he went beyond the Mosaic Law and removed the permission to divorce:

> "It was also said, 'Whoever divorces his wife, let him give her a certificate of divorce.' But I say to you that every one who divorces his wife, except on the ground of unchastity, makes her an adulteress; and whoever marries a divorced woman commits adultery."
>
> — Mt 5:31-32

These are hard words, indeed, as hard as anything John was preaching. Both John and Jesus taught that love of God means following his commandments. As John the apostle says in his first epistle:

> And by this we may be sure that we know him, if we keep his commandments. He who says "I know him" but disobeys his commandments is a liar, and the truth is not in him; but

whoever keeps his word, in him truly love for God is perfected. By this we may be sure that we are in him: he who says he abides in him ought to walk in the same way in which he walked.

— 1 Jn 2:3-6

Following the commandments, and calling others to do so, is not an unloving thing to do. It brings one into alignment with he who is Love . . . God. The commandments were not given to man in order to stifle his freedom or restrict his happiness. No, precisely the opposite. One who lives by them is in harmony both with his Creator and with his fellow man, as is necessary for a fulfilled and joyful life.

One of the unfortunate messages of modern culture is that fulfillment and happiness are found in "breaking the rules" and living out our most base desires. This is no more logical than a cat trying to find joy in flying or a fish trying to fulfill itself by singing. Man was created in the image and likeness of God, was indeed made for God and to live in him. Attempts to find fulfillment by breaking God's commandments lead only to pain — and it is most likely a mercy when that pain happens in *this* life, giving us a reminder of the path that we should follow. Disobedience of God's commandments is the way of death and failure: broken marriages, destruction of the body through drugs, and loneliness unfulfilled in promiscuity. True joy and fulfillment is found in aligning ourselves to the ways of him who is Love.

John the Baptist and Jesus both call each person to "be perfect, as your heavenly Father is perfect" (Mt 5:48). How is this possible? Humanly, it is not. It is only through grace — the gift of God's life — that we are able to live as we ought. Here, again, is something that John prepared for and Jesus fulfilled. When John baptized, his baptism was a public sign of the person's repentance; it was not a sacrament empowered by the saving death and resurrection of Christ. As such, it did not wash away a person's sins. St. John Chrysostom preached:

> John was not bestowing the gift, which was remission of sins, but preparing beforehand the souls of those who would receive the God of all.
>
> — *Gospel of Matthew Homily* 10.3[6]

John's baptism was part of an existing practice of baptism within Judaism, the purpose of which was a public declaration of one's inner repentance. Unlike sacramental baptism, however, it did not give a person grace to live a more perfect life. Any one of his followers who tried to live John's preaching completely would have failed. The power of sin and pull of the flesh are too great. But Jesus took this sign and made it effective. In Christian sacramental baptism, a person is completely forgiven of sin and filled with the grace needed to live a holy life — one that follows the commandments, but even goes beyond them. Through baptism, Jesus gives a person the grace needed even to "be perfect."

What does it mean to be "perfect"? Jesus tells a potential follower of his:

> "If you would be perfect, go, sell what you possess and give to the poor, and you will have treasure in heaven; and come, follow me."
>
> — Mt 19:21

Jesus is telling the rich young man that his disordered attachments to the things of this world are preventing him from loving God above all. But the young man went away sad, because he did not have the power within himself to abandon his life so completely to God. However, baptism imparts the grace a person needs in order to indeed be perfect and follow the Lord completely. This is why Jesus says, "He who is least in the kingdom of heaven is greater than [John the Baptist]" (Mt 11:11). The least

in the kingdom of heaven has received a gift that John did not —
sacramental baptism — and, through this gift, has been born again
into God's kingdom. John's baptism was a preparation, but it is in
the baptism of Christ that the shared message of John and Jesus is
fulfilled and the "kingdom of heaven is at hand."

REFERENCES
Mt 14:2, 16:14

For Reflection
- Do I direct other people to Christ in my words and actions?
- By prayer, or fasting, or rooting out sin, am I preparing
  a way for Christ to enter my heart? Or are my habits and
  prejudices barring the way?

Elijah

"Who do men say that the Son of man is?"
And they said, "Some say . . . Elijah . . ."

In 1970, a book was released which went on to become that decade's nonfiction bestseller and one of the bestselling books of all time. Titled *The Late, Great Planet Earth* and written by Hal Lindsey, this book explained modern events — such as the founding of modern Israel in 1948 and the growing union of European countries — as being clear fulfillments of events that the Bible indicates will be precursors to the Second Coming. The book's conclusion — that interpretation of biblical prophecy proved that Jesus was returning soon — caused a sensation.

Although Lindsey had much greater success in marketing his predictions than most, he was neither the first nor the last Christian to make such claims. Despite Christ's statements that even the angels in heaven do not know the hour of his coming (Mt 24:36), Christians of all types have made it their business to predict the details of Christ's glorious return. Yet, over and over, these predictions come to naught, and many people who were so sure of the signs eventually realize that their confident interpretation was wildly incorrect.

End-of-the-world speculation is not confined to Christians, however. A deep apocalyptic vein runs through Islam, and the Jewish people have been awaiting the Messianic era to mark the end of this world for thousands of years. The Old Testament is full of hints and signs about the coming of the Anointed One, who will inaugurate the new age. Furthermore, this age will be prepared for beforehand, and one of the most prominent preparatory events is that Elijah — who left this world in a whirlwind (2 Kings 2:11) — will return to prepare the world for the coming of the Messiah. The prophet Malachi proclaims this belief in the last words found in the Old Testament:

> "Behold, I will send you Elijah the prophet before the great and terrible day of the LORD comes. And he will turn the hearts of fathers to their children and the hearts of children to their fathers, lest I come and smite the land with a curse."
>
> — Mal 4:5

The devout Jew would find it impossible to think that the Messiah would return without first being introduced to the world by Elijah. Even today, Jews sing a hymn called "Elijah the Prophet" each week during the Havlalah prayers that conclude the Sabbath, expressing their desire that the prophet will return at the end of that day to announce the coming of the Messiah.

With all this in mind, it's easy to see why Elijah plays such a prominent role in Matthew's Gospel. Matthew wrote his work specifically for Jewish converts to Christianity, so he wanted to be sure they understood how Jesus of Nazareth fulfilled all the prophecies concerning the Messiah. Some of Jesus' contemporaries thought that perhaps Jesus was not the Messiah, but rather Elijah himself, coming to announce the true Messiah:

> Now when Jesus came into the district of Caesarea Philippi, he asked his disciples, "Who do men say that the Son of man is?" And they said, "Some say John the Baptist, others say Elijah, and others Jeremiah or one of the prophets."
>
> — Mt 16:13-14

Why would some have thought that Jesus was the second coming of Elijah? There were a number of commonalities between the two in their preaching and life, but one miracle in particular hearkened back to Elijah. In 1 Kings 17:7-24, Elijah asks the widow at Zarephath for bread during the drought. Although the widow has barely enough flour and oil for one loaf, she is able to make bread each day for many days. Then, however, her son becomes ill and dies. In a remarkable instance of God's miraculous power, Elijah beseeches the Lord and raises the widow's son to life. This is one of the greatest miracles told in all the Old Testament, marking Elijah as a singular prophet.

Now advance to the time of Christ: he is entering a town called Nain, where a widow's son has also died. Luke tells the story:

> And he came and touched the bier, and the bearers stood still. And he said, "Young man, I say to you, arise." And the dead man sat up, and began to speak. And he gave him to his mother. Fear seized them all; and they glorified God, saying, "A great prophet has arisen among us!" and "God has visited his people!" And this report concerning him spread through the whole of Judea and all the surrounding country.
>
> — Lk 7:14-17

Who is the "great prophet" that had arisen? In the opinion of many of Christ's contemporaries, it was none other than Elijah himself. Since Elijah had not died (cf. 2 Kings 2:11), it was a common belief in Judaism that his promised return would be literal: he would come from heaven and walk the earth again. Because of Christ's miracles and bold preaching (similar in tone to Elijah's), many Jews concluded that Jesus was, indeed, Elijah returned.

The early Church Fathers — although they, of course, realized that Christ was not a returning Elijah — examined the likeness between the two and were able to find many ways in which Elijah was a type of Christ, meaning that his whole life and his person were reflections of the life and person of Christ. Aphrahat, an Assyrian Christian of the fourth century, wrote:

Elijah . . . was persecuted as Jesus was persecuted. Jezebel the murderess persecuted Elijah; and the persecuting and murderous congregation persecuted Jesus. Elijah restrained the heavens from rain because of the sins of Israel; and Jesus by His coming restrained the Spirit from the prophets, because of the sins of the people. Elijah destroyed the servants of Baal; and Jesus trampled upon Satan and his hosts. Elijah raised to life the son of the widow; and Jesus raised to life the son of the widow, as well as Lazarus and the daughter of the ruler of the Synagogue. Elijah sustained the widow with a little bread; and Jesus satisfied thousands with a little bread. Elijah was taken up in a chariot to heaven; and our Redeemer ascended and took His seat on the right hand of His Father. Elisha received the spirit of Elijah; and Jesus breathed upon the faces of His Apostles.

— *Demonstration* 21:14[7]

More than anything, though, it is their shared persecution that brings together Elijah and Jesus as prophets. Jesus predicts his own persecution during the momentous discussion with his apostles about who he is in Matthew 16. Even though the apostles had come to realize that Jesus transcends Elijah and all mortal men, Jesus quickly disabuses them of any notion that his divine sonship precludes him from sharing in the suffering of the prophets (Mt 16:21). Christ's path to glory lies through the cross, and anyone who rejects that path serves the devil (cf. Mt 16:23). Jesus goes on to promise that his followers will also taste this suffering:

Then Jesus told his disciples, "If any man would come after me, let him deny himself and take up his cross and follow me. For whoever would save his life will lose it, and whoever loses his life for my sake will find it. For what will it profit a man, if he gains the whole world and forfeits his life? Or what shall a man give in return for his life?"

— Mt 16:24-26

The prophet's life is a difficult one, yet all Christians by virtue of their baptism are called to be "priest, prophet, and king" like

Christ. The essence of being a prophet is to tell the truth about God, especially when this truth is challenging to your listeners. The history of the prophets makes clear what the result of this declaration of God's truth is: persecution. Christ himself also declares suffering to be a consequence of being his follower when he says:

> "Blessed are you when men revile you and persecute you and utter all kinds of evil against you falsely on my account. Rejoice and be glad, for your reward is great in heaven, for so men persecuted the prophets who were before you."
>
> — Mt 5:11-12

Later, the apostle John gives a striking image of the privileges and consequences of being a prophet:

> So I went to the angel and told him to give me the little scroll; and he said to me, "Take it and eat; it will be bitter to your stomach, but sweet as honey in your mouth." And I took the little scroll from the hand of the angel and ate it; it was sweet as honey in my mouth, but when I had eaten it my stomach was made bitter. And I was told, "You must again prophesy about many peoples and nations and tongues and kings."
>
> — Rev 10:9-11

The eating of the scroll represents the arrival of the Word of God into the life of the prophet: now, when he speaks, it is God's words that are uttered. This is a delight to the prophet, as he embraces a deep intimacy with the Lord — the scroll is "sweet as honey in my mouth." But the results of the prophet's utterances are most often rejection and persecution; people are too tied to their sinful ways to accept loving reproof. Thus, after proclaiming the Word, the prophet's "stomach was made bitter." Suffering is the inevitable result of the proclamation of the Word.

But Jesus does not promise only persecution for his followers; he also promises that his Holy Spirit will be with them in every difficulty and trial (cf. Mk 13:11). How so? Not in a great flash of lightning, an earthquake, or a vision from heaven. No, the Spirit will be with each disciple in persecution and trial, just as he was with Elijah during his time of suffering: in a "still, small voice" (1 Kings 19:13). Like Elijah, the Christian must listen for this voice of the Spirit, gain strength from it, and accept from it the ability to be a prophetic voice to others. The prophetic voice might be as simple as refusing to join others in gossip, idleness, or crude talk at the workplace, or as difficult as facing political persecution for the Christian faith. Every Christian, however, will endure some share of the sufferings of a prophet if he is faithful to his call.

Christ, of course, endured the sufferings of the prophet, though he was much more than a prophet. If it is apparent that Jesus was not Elijah, returning to announce the Messiah, then who was? Matthew is careful to demonstrate clearly that the great prophet returned in the person of John the Baptist. In Matthew 17:10-13, the following exchange between Jesus and his disciples occurs:

> [T]he disciples asked [Jesus], "Then why do the scribes say that first Elijah must come?" He replied, "Elijah does come, and he is to restore all things; but I tell you that Elijah has already come, and they did not know him, but did to him whatever they pleased. So also the Son of man will suffer at their hands." Then the disciples understood that he was speaking to them of John the Baptist.
>
> — Mt 17:10-13

Matthew likely included this discussion in his Gospel because one of the arguments used by Jews in the first century against Christian claims was that Jesus could not be the Messiah, as Elijah had not yet returned. The evangelist reminded his readers of an important principle: sometimes the fulfillment of God's prophecies does not occur as commonly expected — or even as expected by the prophet himself.

This should not be surprising to the student of the Bible. The Old Testament is full of situations in which prophecies came true, but in an unexpected way. Abraham believed that Ishmael was the son of promise, but God had different plans. God promised Jacob the Patriarch that after he sojourned in Egypt, God would "bring [him] up again" to the Promised Land (Gen 50:24). But Jacob, whom God had renamed "Israel," died in Egypt, yet his people — the nation named after him — were miraculously delivered 400 years later. St. John of the Cross, the great sixteenth-century mystic, gives sage advice regarding the interpretation of prophecy:

> We must not consider a prophecy from the perspective of our perception and language, for God's language is another one, according to the spirit, very different from what we understand, and difficult. This is so true that even Jeremiah, a prophet himself, observing that the ideas in God's words were so different from the meaning people would ordinarily find in them, seems to be beguiled and defends the people: "Alas, alas, alas, Lord God, have you perchance deceived this people and Jerusalem, saying: Peace will come to you; and behold the sword reaches even to the soul?" [Jer 4:10]
>
> — *Ascent of Mount Carmel* 2.19.7[8]

St. John gives example after example from the Scriptures showing how God worked in unexpected ways, even when he had pre-announced his actions!

So it's a dangerous business trying to comprehend the mind of God. This applies not just to prophecy but to all the many and varied ways in which God works in the world and in each person's life. How often do we interpret some event as a definitive statement from God, only to see it in an altogether different light after time passes? Perhaps the lost job, which appears to be a rejection by God of a certain career, was actually a change needed to advance that career. Or the broken relationship that causes such pain and hurt opens the door to meeting our future spouse. We must be careful not to shape the meaning of events by way of our own preconceptions and limited outlook.

To hear the Word of the Lord and be submissive to it requires a poverty of spirit. One of the primary reasons the religious leaders of his time rejected Jesus as Messiah is that they were filled up with their own ideas of what a Messiah ought to be, instead of cultivating an emptiness that would allow God to show them a better path. This emptiness, this poverty, is the outstanding virtue of the first Christians. These men and women knew the prophecies promising a glorious kingdom inaugurated by the Messiah. And probably, like their co-religionists, they had forgotten the prophecies of a suffering Messiah. Yet when Christ came in an unexpected form, they opened their hearts to this reality and embraced it fully. They allowed God to shape their understanding of his plans, instead of rejecting what contradicted their preconceptions.

Consider St. Paul. His whole life was dedicated to the defense of the glory of Israel when he was asked to accept that all of his nation's hopes and dreams rested on a shamefully executed criminal. Yet accept it he did, and in doing so, he began to see how the promises found in the Old Testament were fulfilled by Jesus of Nazareth — not in the way he or his fellow religious leaders expected, but in a much more glorious way.

Being part of 2,000 years of following Christ can lead the Christian to a complacent view of Jesus and his work. The oft-repeated stories — Christ's birth, miracles, death, and resurrection — become familiar tales that fail to capture the heart. Each generation must see Christ's work as ever new, challenging previously accepted ways of conceiving him. Poverty of spirit, such as the first Christians had, opens each believer to the new ways in which the Lord works and speaks, as we trust that he will fulfill his promises in ways unimaginable to our limited outlook. When the cry is made, "Maranatha" — "Come, Lord Jesus!" — we must be ready to receive him as he desires to reveal himself, not as we in our narrow vision desire him to be.

REFERENCES

Mt 16:14

For Reflection

- How can I fulfill the Christian's call to be a prophet?
- Do I proclaim the truth about God, even when it is unfashionable or difficult?
- Do I look for consolation from the Holy Spirit or from the world?

Jeremiah

"Who do men say that the Son of man is?"
And they said, "Some say . . . Jeremiah . . ."

What's the difference between a pessimist and a realist? Usually, the distinction is the outcome of the events forecast — were they less dire than envisioned, or was the negative prediction justified? In the seventh century before Christ, the Jews had what they thought was an exceedingly, even dangerously, pessimistic would-be prophet in their midst.

Jeremiah predicted the unthinkable: the destruction of the holy city of Jerusalem and an end to the kingdom of David. Worse still, he proclaimed that the blame for these events rested squarely with the people themselves: their unfaithfulness to Yahweh would be the cause of their destruction. Many of his listeners felt Jeremiah even seemed to *rejoice* in Israel's coming defeat, leading them to question his patriotism. Never, however, did he allow the crowds' rejection of him to alter the message — that God would humble his unfaithful people to bring them back to covenant faithfulness with him.

Jeremiah's condemnations of Israel sprang from a deep love for God's people. Although it pained him to preach about death and destruction, he knew he must do so in order to lead them back to God. Only much later, after events unfolded exactly as he predicted, was Jeremiah proclaimed by Israel as a true prophet of God who gave a realistic (not a pessimistic) view into the future.

It might be difficult today to see a similarity between this harsh Old Testament figure and Jesus of Nazareth. John the Baptist could perhaps be considered another Jeremiah, but not the man who proclaimed himself as "gentle" (Mt 11:29) and exalted the "meek" (Mt 5:5). Yet, to the people who encountered Jesus directly, there was clearly a likeness. When Jesus asks, "Who do men say that the Son of man is?" (Mt 16:13), the apostles recount the various things they have heard during Christ's ministry: "Some say John the Baptist, others say Elijah, and others Jeremiah or one of the prophets" (Mt 16:14). Clearly, then, at least some people who had heard Jesus preach were reminded of the figure of Jeremiah and believed he had come to continue that mission.

The common image that prevails today of Jesus — a mild preacher of peace and harmony — was not the perception of those who encountered him; instead, many saw him as the figure of a prophet who could be a divisive preacher of God's wrath. In his denunciations of the money-changers or the hypocrisy of the religious leaders, Jesus — like Jeremiah — wanted to make clear that God's love can be likened to a consuming fire: purifying those who love him, but terrifying to those who reject him.

It is unlikely, then, that any of Christ's contemporaries would have composed a hymn in his honor titled "Gentle Jesus, Meek and Mild." Instead, Jesus' image in his own time apparently prompted comparisons to a passionate Old Testament prophet, not a milquetoast figure preaching peace and harmony. And the fire behind both men was the same: a deep desire to see sinners reconciled to God.

It is in the twenty-third chapter of Matthew that Jesus most clearly appears as the fulfillment of the Old Testament prophets like Jeremiah. First, he proclaims seven "woes" upon the leaders of Israel, not sparing them from any of his wrath. He calls them "blind fools" (Mt 23:17), "whitewashed tombs" (Mt 23:27), and "hypocrites" (Mt 23:13ff). Their hypocrisy especially is singled out for condemnation, and Jesus does nothing to soften the blow of his denunciation. Yet, at the end of his polemic, he makes it clear that all of his fury is impelled by deep love:

> "O Jerusalem, Jerusalem, killing the prophets and stoning those who are sent to you! How often would I have gathered your children together as a hen gathers her brood under her wings, and you would not!"
>
> — Mt 23:37

This motherly, tender love is striking juxtaposed to his condemnations, but it is this love that has produced these harsh words. It is this love that drove both Jeremiah and Jesus to rage without compromise against sin and unfaithfulness.

The Church has always seen Old Testament figures and events as prefiguring the person and life of Jesus, and the figure of Jeremiah is no exception. Theodore of Mopsuestia, a great Scripture scholar of the fourth century, saw the connection between Jeremiah and Jesus when he wrote:

> In the same way they had supposed that Christ was Jeremiah. Perhaps they knew that the Lord had wisdom from his birth and was without peer in his teaching. Something similar was thought of Jeremiah, in that as a child he was singled out for prophecy and that without human training he was the prophet of a greater prophet to follow.
>
> — *Fragment* 91[9]

Theodore recognized that Jeremiah's life was a foreshadowing of the life that Jesus would live.

God's people have long understood that there are certain "rhythms" to how God works in salvation history: how he worked with our fathers will be similar to how he works today with us. Like a garden that has been lovingly tended over the years by a master gardener, the soil has become ready to accept new seed and nurture it to fruition. Knowing how God works in the past allows his followers to anticipate how he will work in the present and the future. Christ is the fulfillment of all Old Testament prophets; their words are foreshadowings of him and his work. He completes that work of the Father to which Jeremiah and the other prophets pointed.

The first of the many aspects of Jeremiah's life that prefigure Jesus can be found, as Theodore noted, even before Jeremiah's birth. Like Jesus, he was destined by God in the womb for a prophetic mission.

> "Before I formed you in the womb I knew you, and before you were born I consecrated you; I appointed you a prophet to the nations."
>
> — Jer 1:5

Once Jeremiah begins his mission, he — like Jesus — is mistreated by those in religious authority, has enemies who plot his death, predicts the fall of the temple, and sheds tears over the eventual destruction of Jerusalem. Jeremiah also shares with the coming Messiah a disinterest in political liberation and preaches instead a spiritual liberation. Jeremiah's words describing himself — "a lamb led to the slaughter" (Jer 11:19) — can clearly be used also of Christ.

But the deepest connection between the two is shared suffering. Contrary to the popular opinion of the time, Jeremiah does not rejoice in Israel's imminent destruction. It pains him greatly; it seems that Jeremiah physically suffers the pain that he predicts in Israel's future. Part of the "job description" of all the prophets was suffering for their people. Today's common view of a prophet as a self-appointed judge, reveling in his supposed moral superiority, couldn't be further from the truth about the prophets of Israel. Jeremiah and all the prophets recognize that true fulfillment could only come from being conformed to the ways of God. Rejecting his laws and being unfaithful to his covenant leads only to misery and death. Jeremiah weeps over this misery, desiring only that the people of God might be reconciled to the Maker who created them for eternal enjoyment of him.

Frustration was a significant part of the suffering of all the Old Testament prophets. For all their calls to repentance, they had no ability to change the fundamental state of relationship between God and man. The pull of sin and its offspring, death, still plagued the human race, and nothing a prophet could do would change that. This was not the case with Jesus, however. Although he was part of their prophetic tradition, he did what none of them could do: he took the sin, misery, and death of his people upon himself and allowed it to be crucified on Calvary. He did not merely have empathy with his people; he truly "became sin" (2 Cor 5:21) for them so that the power of sin might be destroyed. And at the root of all his actions was the desire for the reconciliation of sinners to his Father in heaven.

Beyond these prefigurements in Jeremiah's life, another event involving the great prophet also pointed the way to Christ. In 2 Maccabees, it is written that Jeremiah hid the Ark of the Covenant:

> Jeremiah came and found a cave, and he brought there the tent and the ark and the altar of incense, and he sealed up the entrance. Some of those who followed him came up to mark the way, but could not find it. When Jeremiah learned of it, he rebuked them and declared: "The place shall be unknown until God gathers his people together again and shows his mercy. And then the Lord will disclose these things, and the glory of the Lord and the cloud will appear, as they were shown in the case of Moses, and as Solomon asked that the place should be specially consecrated."
>
> — 2 Macc 2:5-8

Jeremiah foresaw that the Ark of the Covenant would only be revealed in the Messianic Age, when "God gathers his people together." Because of his prophecy, there was great anticipation among the Jewish people regarding the discovery of the Ark. If, in Jesus' time, this hallowed artifact had been discovered, it would have caused a spectacular celebration among the Jewish people. It would have been seen as a harbinger of Israel's liberation from her oppressors — namely, Rome. However, what the first-century Jews didn't realize was that a new covenant, one that would fulfill and even supersede the old, was standing in their midst. This new covenant had a new Ark: a peasant girl from Nazareth, who accepted her role with a simple "Let it be to me according to your word" (Lk 1:38). The old ark made of wood was no longer necessary, for the new ark brought forth Jesus, who was instituting a new relationship between God and his people, one in which the law would no longer reside on tablets of stone.

Ironically, it was to Jeremiah that this was revealed centuries beforehand, since he prophesied about the coming of Jesus and the covenant he would establish:

> "Behold, the days are coming, says the LORD, when I will make a new covenant with the house of Israel and the house of Judah, not like the covenant which I made with their fathers when I took them by the hand to bring them out of the land of Egypt, my covenant which they broke, though I was their husband, says the LORD. But this is the covenant which I will make with the house of Israel after those days, says the LORD: I will put my law within them, and I will write it upon their hearts; and I will be their God, and they shall be my people. And no longer shall each man teach his neighbor and each his brother, saying, 'Know the LORD,' for they shall all know me, from the least of them to the greatest, says the LORD; for I will forgive their iniquity, and I will remember their sin no more."
>
> — Jer 31:31-34

The Law was the centerpiece of the Jewish religion; because of it, the Chosen People were unique among all the nations of the world. By this divine gift given to Moses, the Israelites were able to know the ways of God and how to follow him. Jeremiah, however, saw that the day would come when his people would have written on their hearts a divine law that would allow them to truly know the Lord and to be cleansed from their sins. The Law, so wondrously given on Mt. Sinai with signs and power, would now be given to all God's people, from the greatest to the least, in the secret of their hearts. Jeremiah himself must have been astounded at his own prophecy, as it went so far beyond anything an ancient Israelite could conceive.

But how could God write his law upon our hearts? Another great prophet, Ezekiel, describes how this transformation would take place:

> "Thus says the Lord GOD . . . I will sprinkle clean water upon you, and you shall be clean from all your uncleannesses, and from all your idols I will cleanse you. A new heart I will give you, and a new spirit I will put within you; and I will take out of your flesh the heart of stone and give you a heart of flesh. And I will put my spirit within you, and cause you to walk in my statutes and be careful to observe my ordinances."
>
> — Ezek 36:22, 25-27

This "clean water" of God predicted by Ezekiel is marvelously fulfilled in the sacrament of Baptism — since through it, God mystically transforms the recipient's heart of stone into a heart filled with grace and love. As God wrote the Old Law on stone tablets, he now writes his new law on stony hearts, transforming them into hearts of fire. Baptism makes its recipient into another Ark of the Covenant, as each who receives it carries God's law of love within his heart. No longer is God's covenant hidden in a cave; now it resides in every baptized believer. And not only does God's law reside therein, but also his very life — grace that gives believers the ability to follow that law.

Jeremiah said that in the new covenant each man shall "know the LORD." This is not the knowledge that resides in the mind, but the knowledge that lies deep in the heart: an intimate, true knowledge, as between a husband and wife. A knowledge that leads one to follow God's laws not out of fear or obligation, but out of love. A knowledge that transforms the believer's whole life into the very image and likeness of God, and fosters a desire for his glory above all things. This knowledge was prophesied by Jeremiah, fulfilled by Jesus, and begins in each person through baptism in the clean waters of God.

REFERENCES
Mt 16:14

For Reflection
- Is my image of Jesus one that is safe and comfortable?
- Do I allow Jesus to call me to repentance in my life?
- Does my knowledge of the Lord change the way I live?

King of the Jews

"Are you the King of the Jews?"

Two millennia ago, an obscure man was designated "King of the Jews" by the Romans. He was not accepted as such by the Jews themselves for two reasons: he had roots in an unacceptable, less "pure" part of Israel, and his actions violated so many of their deeply held beliefs. His name, however, has been remembered throughout the ages, and his actions played a pivotal role in salvation history. That man is King Herod the Great.

Herod was born around 73 B.C. to an Arabian mother and a father from Idumea, a region whose inhabitants were believed by pious Jews to be racially impure. Eusebius of Caesarea was to see Herod's foreign lineage as the fulfillment of prophecy:

> When Herod, the first ruler of foreign blood, became King, the prophecy of Moses received its fulfillment, according to which there should "not be wanting a prince of Judah, nor a ruler from his loins, until he come for whom it is reserved" [Gen 49:10]. This prediction remained unfulfilled so long as it was permitted them to live under rulers from their own nation, that is, from the time of Moses to the reign of Augustus. Under the latter, Herod, the first foreigner, was given the Kingdom of the Jews by the Romans.
>
> — *History of the Church* 1.6.1 [10]

Herod's father, Antipater, was involved in Roman politics, and was eventually poisoned due to his support of Caesar's murderers. Herod, however, was able to convince the Empire of his loyalty and rose in the ranks, until being named "King of the Jews" by the

Roman Senate in 40 B.C. During his reign, he was renowned for his architectural projects, such as fortresses at Masada and Herodium. But no undertaking was more ambitious than the expansion of the Jerusalem temple, a task that lasted over eighty years, long after his death.

Ironically, King Herod is best known today for his terrible action, now known as the Massacre of the Holy Innocents, surrounding the birth of a future king in Bethlehem. Wise men had come from the East and asked Herod, "Where is he who has been born king of the Jews? For we have seen his star in the East, and have come to worship him" (Mt 2:2). To Herod, this was subversive — nothing less than a direct challenge to his kingship, a challenge that could not go unanswered. In fact, Herod had previously had even family members murdered when he believed them to be potential usurpers to his throne. His response in this instance was no less brutal: he ordered the murder of all male children under two years of age in Bethlehem — thus, according to Matthew, fulfilling Jeremiah's prophecy:

> "A voice was heard in Ramah,
> wailing and loud lamentation,
> Rachel weeping for her children;
> she refused to be consoled,
> because they were no more."

> — Mt 2:18

Since its earliest days, the Church has seen in these infant victims the first martyrs for Christ. On the Feast of the Holy Innocents, the Church expresses the depth of their sacrifice:

> These children cry out their praises to the Lord; by their death they have proclaimed what they could not preach with their infant voices.
> — Antiphon 2, Morning Prayer, Feast of the Holy Innocents

The actions of Herod reveal the template for Roman dealings with the Jews in the time of Christ. The Empire's presence always lingers in the background in the Gospels, ever threatening to erupt in violence.

In general, the Romans were tolerant of the Jews, allowing them many privileges not accorded to other occupied peoples. Yet on one point, they were brutally direct: they would allow no challenge to their political authority. Only when Jewish claims seemed to intrude on their power did they intervene, but when they did, it was decisive. In this case, Herod makes clear that he will reject any conjecture of another "King of the Jews," even if it is a fulfillment of some Hebrew prophecy.

Christ's life, which in general did not intersect directly with Roman rule, is nevertheless bookended by encounters with Roman officials. Already we have seen how Herod dealt with his birth; at the end of Christ's life, another Roman official would decide his fate. In Matthew 27:11-14, this man, Pontius Pilate, interrogates Jesus. His first question, "Are you the King of the Jews?" (Mt 27:11), reveals his overriding concern: not some debates about provincial religious customs, but threats to the existing political order.

Pilate, like Herod before him and most politicians of any age, could not conceive of anything more important than political power. One either had power or could be abused by power — in the view of such men, there is no other option. All else was subservient to this issue.

It is clear that this was also the outlook of his guards. They mockingly clothed Christ as a king and called out, "Hail, King of the Jews!" (Mt 27:29). The sarcastic title given to him by those in power becomes his epitaph: "This is Jesus, the King of the Jews" (Mt 27:37). To the Romans, he was nothing other than a pretender to their authority, a pitiful excuse for a king.

Yet in truth, Jesus is a king, a king of an altogether different sort than King Herod the Great. Indeed, their kingships are a study in contrasts. Herod spent great energy erecting imposing physical structures, built with stone and brick; Christ was committed to building the Church, founded on poor fishermen and laborers. Herod clung to his power jealously, eliminating any claimants to his throne, real or imagined. Christ, on the other hand, willingly gave himself up to death, not clinging to his power as the Son of God. The results of their respective kingships are ironic. Herod died a painful death, and his kingdom didn't even outlive him: his territory was divided into three parts under his three surviving sons. Even his greatest project, the expansion of the Temple, came to naught when it was completely destroyed in 70 A.D., shortly after the renovations he started were completed. Yet the power Herod served, the Roman Empire, would 300 years later declare the babe of Bethlehem as the King of the Universe. Emperors would pledge allegiance to him who died a disgraced criminal under their predecessors' rule. And, after the destruction of this "everlasting" Roman rule, Christ would still reign as the king over the hearts of billions throughout the world. He who grasped power lost it; he who willingly humbled himself gained it.

This is the logic of the Gospel, and the instances of the title "King of the Jews" in Matthew reflect this fundamental quality of Christ's kingship. Notice that the term is used during the two moments when Christ most humbles himself: at his birth as a baby in a humble manger, and at his death as a condemned criminal. The self-humbling of Christ was considered so important to the first Christians that it was exalted in a hymn that Paul includes in his letter to the Philippians:

> [Christ] emptied himself, taking the form of a servant, being born in the likeness of men. And being found in human form he humbled himself and became obedient unto death, even death on a cross.
>
> — Phil 2:7-8

Christ's first "emptying" was his becoming man — "taking the form of a servant"; his second, further "emptying" was his disgraceful death — "even death on a cross" — for our salvation. Christ, as the eternal Son of God, had every prerogative and privilege of God. Yet he gladly gave up all those privileges for our sake. As Paul says elsewhere: "Though he was rich, yet for your sake he became poor, so that by his poverty you might become rich" (2 Cor 8:9). Another translation could be "he became a beggar"; Christ's self-abnegation was so complete that he gave up everything to fulfill his Father's will. The purpose of Christ's self-willed poverty is this: our reception of the riches of heaven. His descent he willed for our ascent.

But Christ's poverty is not the end of the story. Paul rejoices in the consequences of this dual self-emptying:

> Therefore God has highly exalted him and bestowed on him the name which is above every name, that at the name of Jesus every knee should bow, in heaven and on earth and under the earth, and every tongue confess that Jesus Christ is Lord, to the glory of God the Father.
>
> — Phil 2:9-11

Because he did not cling to power, but emptied himself, Christ is made king of all — Jews and Gentiles. This kingdom is glorious beyond all imagination, making Herod's or even Caesar's kingdom pale in comparison. The apostle John saw a vision of the awesome power of this eternal kingship in his Apocalypse:

> Then I saw heaven opened, and behold, a white horse! He who sat upon it is called Faithful and True, and in righteousness he judges and makes war. His eyes are like a flame of fire, and on his head are many diadems; and he has a name inscribed which no one knows but himself. He is clad in a robe dipped in blood, and the name by which he is called is The Word of God. And the armies of heaven, arrayed in fine linen, white and pure, followed him on white horses. From his mouth issues a sharp sword with which to smite the nations, and he will rule them

with a rod of iron; he will tread the wine press of the fury of the wrath of God the Almighty. On his robe and on his thigh he has a name inscribed, King of kings and Lord of lords.

— Rev 19:11-16

Christ's model of ascending to his throne through self-emptying becomes the model for all of his followers. It is only through humbling ourselves — becoming "empty" of selfish passions, desires, and possessions — that we are exalted with Christ. The eventual exaltation of the poor by God is a common theme in the Old Testament, as seen in Hannah's prayer of praise to the Lord:

"He raises up the poor from the dust; he lifts the needy from the ash heap, to make them sit with princes and inherit a seat of honor."

— 1 Sam 2:8

This expectation of the exaltation of the poor and humble is also seen in Mary's *Magnificat*:

"He has put down the mighty from their thrones, and exalted those of low degree; he has filled the hungry with good things, and the rich he has sent empty away."

— Lk 1:52-53

God will lift up those who imitate his Son by being poor; yet he will also "put down the mighty from their thrones." Those who cling to power, like Herod, will be humbled; if not in this life, then in the next. Notice the irony in what God does to the rich: he sends them "empty away." Thus, each person will be emptied: it will either be a self-emptying, in which one chooses Christ as his fulfillment; or it will be God's wrathful emptying, in which those who reject him are denied the riches of his kingdom. There can be only one king allowed in each man's heart: it is either self or Christ. A good subject in any kingdom models himself after the King, and in the kingdom of heaven, it is no different. Each follower of Christ must imitate him and empty himself; in doing so, he will be glorified with Christ one day in heaven.

How do we empty ourselves? How do we imitate the king? Christ tells his followers the practical application of how to serve the king in his fearsome explanation of the king's judgment on his subjects:

> "Truly, I say to you, as you did it to one of the least of these my brethren, you did it to me. . . . Truly, I say to you, as you did it not to one of the least of these, you did it not to me."
>
> — Mt 25:40, 45

This is the heart of emptiness: the good of others always precedes the good of self. The mother who gives of herself, day in and day out, for her children; the parish priest who quietly spends his life's energy for the good of his flock; the nurse who heroically cares for the infirm and disabled: all these are models of self-emptying, and like Christ, God will exalt these over the rich and powerful of this world. The Gospel is a subversive message; it upends existing powers and lifts up the unwanted and the rejected. Serving those who need help most — the poor, the imprisoned, the handicapped, the unborn — requires that one subjugate his privileges and rights for the good of others. Christ had all the privileges of the eternal Son of God, yet he gave them all up in his birth and death for the good of others. He requires the subjects of his kingdom to do the same.

REFERENCES
Mt 2:2, 27:11, 27:29, 27:37

For Reflection
- What actions can I take to place others above myself in my family, friendships, or workplace?
- How might I grow in humility? Do I really want to?

Prophet

"This is the prophet Jesus from Nazareth of Galilee."

In the darkest hour of the darkest century of human existence, one man single-handedly led his country against the forces of an evil empire. Winston Churchill rallied the English and helped them to stand against the Nazi threat, eventually leading England to victory over Germany in World War II. He was hailed the world over as the savior of the English people and the indefatigable enemy of the forces of fascism. Surprisingly enough, however, Churchill resoundingly lost his bid for reelection shortly after the war's conclusion. The man revered around the world was not able to defeat Clement Attlee in the race for Prime Minister of England. For all his popularity and his efforts to protect England, just months after Hitler's defeat, the populace no longer felt he was the right man to lead them.

Churchill's story is but one historical example of mankind's fickleness. Those who appear on top of the world are rejected by the crowds, often for no discernible reason, the next day. Fashions come and go, opinions shift like the wind: it would seem that it is the prerogative of the masses to change their minds at the smallest provocation.

In the Gospels, it's clear that Jesus reaches the heights of his popularity on Palm Sunday. Matthew recounts the scene, one that must have remained vivid in the apostles' minds:

> [T]hey brought the ass and the colt, and put their garments on them, and [Jesus] sat thereon. Most of the crowd spread their

garments on the road, and others cut branches from the trees and spread them on the road. And the crowds that went before him and that followed him shouted, "Hosanna to the Son of David! Blessed is he who comes in the name of the Lord! Hosanna in the highest!" And when he entered Jerusalem, all the city was stirred, saying, "Who is this?" And the crowds said, "This is the prophet Jesus from Nazareth of Galilee."

— Mt 21:7-11

Jerusalem was in a state of excitement unlike anything since the Maccabean Revolt, almost 200 years prior; Jesus was looked upon as a messenger from God, a prophet who would usher in a new kingdom. The crowds praised him as the son of David, the greatest king in Israelite history. But to many in the crowd, Jesus was also the fulfillment of the prophecy of Moses:

"The LORD your God will raise up for you a prophet like me from among you, from your brethren — him you shall heed."

— Deut 18:15

Israel had been looking forward to the fulfillment of this prophecy for generations, hoping for the appearance of "a prophet like [Moses]." Not even Isaiah and Elijah were considered a fulfillment of this prophecy. After the ascension of Christ, Peter was to declare that this prophecy was fulfilled with the coming of Jesus:

"Moses said, 'The Lord God will raise up for you a prophet from your brethren as he raised me up. You shall listen to him in whatever he tells you. And it shall be that every soul that does not listen to that prophet shall be destroyed from the people.' And all the prophets who have spoken, from Samuel and those who came afterwards, also proclaimed these days."

— Acts 3:22-24

What is interesting about this promise, however, is that Moses is not typically looked upon as a prophet; instead, he is traditionally seen as the lawgiver *par excellence*. Yet not considering him as also a prophet is to put a dichotomy between the law and the prophets where one doesn't exist, to separate what is actually a unified whole. The prophets' principal mission is to tell the truth about God, and the Law given through Moses was the primary means by which ancient Israel knew about God: his justice, his mercy, and his holiness. The Old Testament prophets consistently preached that the people must return to a faithful practice of the Law given to Moses. The Law and the prophets were intimately linked in the Jewish religion, and Christ does nothing to separate them in his own preaching; in fact, he proclaims that he does not desire to abolish "the law and the prophets," but to fulfill them both (cf. 5:17).

Throughout his Gospel, Matthew makes an effort to paint Jesus as the "new Moses," one even greater than the first, and the lives of these two men share many commonalities. Moses had to escape death as an infant, as did the baby Jesus. The first Moses went to a mountain to receive the law from God; the new Moses, Jesus, went to a mountain to give the new law from God, the Beatitudes (Mt 5:1-12). On the mountain, Moses' face shone like the sun after his encounter with God; Christ's whole body shone brightly on the mountain of transfiguration. Moses was a law-giving prophet; the crowds on Palm Sunday recognize Jesus as the new law-giving prophet.

Yet we all know how the week that began on Palm Sunday would end. The crowds who praise Jesus as a prophet and sing Hosanna would, a few days later, shout, "Let him be crucified" (Mt 27:22). The support of the people was a mile wide but only an inch deep. As soon as the Pharisees led popular opinion to turn against Jesus, the crowds were all too willing to send him to his death. Jesus, who did nothing to curry favor with the people, doesn't waver on his path in order to gain their friendship in the end.

The lives of the saints, too, reflect the fickleness of public support for those who courageously preach the prophetic truth. St. Athanasius is a particularly apt case study. A bishop at a young age, he tirelessly preached against the fourth-century Arian heresy, which denied the divinity of Christ and had swept over the Roman Empire like a plague. Athanasius staunchly defended the decrees set at the Council of Nicaea, which condemned Arianism — but because the political winds of the time tended to blow Arian, many of the bishops who initially supported Nicaea and the orthodox faith wavered in their support. Not Athanasius. He didn't regard popular consensus as having the power to change what the Holy Spirit decreed through the Church. The phrase "*Athanasius contra mundum*" — "Athanasius against the world" — was indeed fitting for him: five times, the emperor exiled him for refusing to back down against the Arian onslaught; five times, he remained faithful to true Christian doctrine. Eventually, he was restored to his Alexandrian see and permanently vindicated; the orthodox faith prevailed, and he is considered the first Doctor of the Church.

More than a saint, Athanasius was a prophet: he proclaimed the truth about God, regardless of the consequences. Like all the prophets, he drew this strength from his foundation in the Word of God, the never-changing standard by which he discerned truth or falsehood. A prophet recognizes his own failings and weaknesses, and so he clings to the fixed Word of God all the more. Athanasius, fervently embracing the truth of Christ's divinity, could be confident in the standard that he followed.

This highlights perhaps the most important virtue for living the prophetic life of a saint, as St. Theresa of Ávila attests:

> Those who want to journey on this road and continue until they reach the end, which is to drink from this water of life . . . they must have a great and very resolute determination to persevere until reaching the end, come what may, happen what may, whatever work is involved, whatever criticism arises, whether they arrive, or whether they die on the road, or even if they don't have courage for the trials that are met, or if the whole world collapses.
>
> — *Way of Perfection* 21.2[11]

Perseverance is a prerequisite for being a Christian; without it, we become like the seed that cannot take root in the soil (cf. Mt 13:1-8). Instead, we must strive to plant ourselves deep in the soil of the Word of God, gaining strength to withstand temptation, persecution, and tribulation; and not only to withstand them, but to grow a "hundredfold" in the faith.

The model of perseverance is Jesus, who from the beginning knew the mission of his Father and would not be deterred from it: neither the flattery of the crowds, nor the pressure from his own disciples, nor the threats from the religious and political leaders could change his course. He persevered through every hardship and temptation. It's a mistake, however, to believe that following the Father was easy for Christ because he was the divine Son of God. The agony Jesus experienced in Gethsemane (cf. Mt 26:36-46) puts to rest any thought that accomplishing the Father's will was not a struggle for him; it is no less a struggle for each Christian to fulfill the Father's will for their lives.

The perseverance needed during great trials is born of forbearance in everyday hardships. "If any man would come after me, let him deny himself and take up his cross *daily* and follow me" (Lk 9:23 emphasis added). Every day, we can experience martyrdom through all the slight instances of suffering each day brings: enduring the small offenses of others, denying our personal desires for the sake of the good of family or friends, and serving others in small daily, perhaps unseen, tasks. These actions, the fruit of a persistent life of prayer and devotion, are what make possible the ability to stand strong in the face of overwhelming opposition.

"You have been faithful over a little, I will set you over much" (Mt 25:21), Christ said to the man with five talents. By dying to self in small, everyday affairs, we gain strength to die to self in times of great persecution and strife. When everyone else preaches conformity to the world and its passions, the Christian continues to be founded on the Word of God, Jesus Christ. When worn down by the temptations of this world, we who desire to be saints must turn to Christ and ask for a share in the perseverance the Lord had in following the Father's will.

Achieving any goal does not exclude failure; it presupposes it. After countless unsuccessful attempts to create a light bulb, Thomas Edison said, "I have not failed. I've just found 10,000 ways that won't work." The key is rising back up after each fall. Six years after Churchill's defeat, he ran again and was reelected to the post of Prime Minister. Even though he had fallen, he simply got back up and persevered. This is the lot of those who wish to be saints as well. John of Karpathos said:

> Do all in your power not to fall, for the strong athlete should not fall. But if you do fall, get up again at once and continue the contest. Even if you fall a thousand times because of the withdrawal of God's grace, rise up again each time, and keep on doing this until the day of your death. For it is written, "If a righteous man falls down seven times" — that is, repeatedly throughout his life — "seven times shall he rise again" [Prov 24:16].
>
> *— The Philokalia: the Complete Text, Volume I*[12]

It is love of God that inspires us to proclaim Christ to the world prophetically. But without perseverance like that modeled extraordinarily by St. Athanasius, we can endure neither the trials of day-to-day life nor the more significant suffering for which those trials prepare us. Daily conforming ourselves to the One who, though unchangeable, was proclaimed a prophet on Palm Sunday and a criminal on Good Friday, we will find a steadfast, never-failing support against the winds of the world.

REFERENCES

Mt 13:57, 21:11, 21:46

For Reflection

- Have I set spiritual goals that I subsequently gave up on? Why?
- What is keeping me from trying again?

Lord of the Sabbath

"For the Son of man is lord of the Sabbath."

In the classic Mark Twain tale "A Connecticut Yankee in King Arthur's Court," a nineteenth-century Hartford, Connecticut, resident named Hank Morgan is transported back to the land of King Arthur and the Knights of the Round Table. A central theme of the story is the dichotomy between life in nineteenth-century America and life in the time of King Arthur. The contrast reaches a climax when Morgan narrowly escapes being burnt at the stake — but only by successfully predicting a solar eclipse he had learned about in his own time, leading the crowd to believe he has strange and wonderful powers.

Twain's tale was the forerunner of a whole genre of time-travel stories that highlight the clash between modern society and past times. Most typically in such stories, it is the inhabitants of the past who are unable to comprehend future cultures and mores. However, it is just as true that ancient cultures can seem unintelligible to modern eyes. Readers who fail to see or give import to the fundamental differences between modern culture and that of the Bible will fail to fully comprehend the Bible's messages.

One aspect of Jewish culture that the modern viewpoint finds most inexplicable is the complex array of laws regulating every aspect of societal and even familial life, laws to which entire books of the Bible are devoted. Foremost among these regulations are those surrounding the Sabbath, and the importance of this day of rest in the ancient Jewish world cannot be overstated. For the Jewish community, life revolved around this day, the constant, ever-recurring reminder that their God was the God of all creation. The practice of the Sabbath impacted every person in the community — priest, freeman, or slave.

The teaching on the Sabbath was formalized in the time of the Exodus. After God delivers the Israelites out of bondage in the land of Egypt, he begins to form them as a people marked for him and separated from the rest of the pagan world. The primary means of this setting-apart is the Law, which has its center in the Ten Commandments given to Moses on Mount Sinai. Most of these commandments are simply reiterations of the natural law — restrictions on behavior that all men know in their hearts is wrong. One commandment, however, is especially peculiar in that it is not a prohibition of a particular behavior but is the institution of a way of life:

> Remember the sabbath day, to keep it holy. Six days you shall labor, and do all your work; but the seventh day is a sabbath to the LORD your God; in it you shall not do any work, you, or your son, or your daughter, your manservant, or your maidservant, or your cattle, or the sojourner who is within your gates; for in six days the LORD made heaven and earth, the sea, and all that is in them, and rested the seventh day; therefore the LORD blessed the sabbath day and hallowed it.
>
> —Ex 20:8-11

Recalling the story of creation, the Jews are to set apart the seventh day of the week as a day of rest from labor, specifically consecrating it as "holy" and directed toward God.

The Sabbath's purpose is twofold. It ensures, first of all, that God has a privileged place in the life of his people, lest they get so consumed in their daily work that they forget him who is the center of their existence. By being forced to lift their eyes above their world each week, they are reminded that God created them and gave them the gifts of creation. Every seventh day is devoted to worshipping the all-providing God.

Secondly, the Sabbath is meant to establish a balanced relationship between man and the created world. After the Fall, man's work was cursed (Gen 3:17-19), and all his labor became burdensome. Every seventh day, though, God relieves him from his labors, allowing him to enjoy the good world he lives in. According to the Sabbath laws, even animals and the land itself should rest — all of creation pauses each week to give praise to its Creator. Every 50 years (seven times seven years), a "Jubilee year" was declared, in which the entire year was devoted to resting the land, forgiving debts, and freeing those in slavery.

The Fall cursed man's relationship with the land — "thorns and thistles it shall bring forth to you" (Gen 3:18) — but the Sabbath reminds man what his relationship with creation was like before the Fall. The Sabbath rest is thus a beautiful gift from God: it prioritizes man's spiritual life properly by placing God at the center of life, and it orders his physical life as well by giving his week a built-in time of rest.

The continued value of the Sabbath rest in today's world should be obvious. While the contemporary *zeitgeist* promises that life will be better if we are all "connected" to our work at all times, the primary result of our connectedness is not the simplicity and efficiency we were assured but a nonstop workweek and an unrelenting burden of labor. Far from being able to detach ourselves from our work for rest, we are expected to be constantly available for the furthering of corporate America. No longer is time set aside that is disconnected from work and devoted solely to God and his creation. For some, the stress of the modern lifestyle is unmanageable, leading to divorce, drug addiction, and even suicide. Even when the effects are not so dramatic, the unceasing life of work still has its negative impacts: a lack of time for prayer, an inability to endure silence, or less time for interaction with family, friends, and neighbors. The need for regular rest is as relevant today as it ever has been. Although the Sabbath is a product of an ancient culture, its importance remains.

In Christ's time, however, many of the leaders of the Jewish people had twisted the gift of this rejuvenating rest into a burdensome obligation. Over the years they had created so many laws regarding exactly what was and what was not allowed on the Sabbath that for the average Jew it was as much a burden to "rest" on the Sabbath as it was to work. Instead of focusing on the dual purpose of the Sabbath — worshiping God and being in harmony with his creation — these leaders focused on the exact amount of work allowed. Jesus desires that his listeners know the original reason for the Sabbath, but he also looks to elevate the day of rest even beyond its initial intention:

> At that time Jesus went through the grainfields on the sabbath; his disciples were hungry, and they began to pluck heads of grain and to eat. But when the Pharisees saw it, they said to him, "Look, your disciples are doing what is not lawful to do on the sabbath." He said to them, "Have you not read what David did, when he was hungry, and those who were with him: how he entered the house of God and ate the bread of the Presence, which it was not lawful for him to eat nor for those who were with him, but only for the priests? Or have you not read in the law how on the sabbath the priests in the temple profane the sabbath, and are guiltless? I tell you, something greater than the temple is here. And if you had known what this means, 'I desire mercy, and not sacrifice,' you would not have condemned the guiltless. For the Son of man is lord of the sabbath."
>
> — Mt 12:1-9

The Sabbath was given to man to help him be elevated to God, but Jesus, as the Incarnate God, is now the only way to the Father. Instead of just a day to draw us closer to God, we now have a person — Jesus Christ. Rules surrounding the Sabbath must be subjugated to the person of Christ.

Some people would interpret this new reality as meaning an end for laws and rules, but this would be a misunderstanding of Christ's attitude toward the just regulations that were part of

Jewish life, including many of those relating to the Sabbath. Rules and regulations can remind man of higher values, and the Sabbath can be a beautiful way to honor God and his creation. Jesus has no desire to abolish the Sabbath; rather, he wants it to be properly understood and lived.

But by declaring himself the "Lord of the Sabbath," Jesus transcends its original meaning; he desires to reconfigure in a new way this day set aside for the Lord. Some Jews of the time believed that even God was bound to follow the Sabbath rest, and that he still "rested" each seventh day. But Jesus reminds the people that the Sabbath, even though it is a beautiful gift, is not the highest law; the Sabbath was instituted to help man serve God — not so that man, much less God, would serve the Law. God is above all things, even the Sabbath.

Christ's second purpose is more radical. Throughout his Gospel, Matthew demonstrates that Jesus is not only the "new Moses" but that he even supersedes Moses. Like Moses going up the mountain to receive the Law, Jesus ascends the mountain to declare the law of his kingdom during the Sermon on the Mount. Christ declares the superiority of this new law over the Law of Moses by repeatedly stating, "You have heard that it was said . . . but I say to you . . ." Thus, he shows his authority even over Moses. By declaring the "Son of Man" — himself — as the "Lord of the Sabbath," he links himself directly to the Creator of the Sabbath and the object of Sabbath worship; he makes his own person the central figure of true Sabbath worship of God, a reconfiguration of the Sabbath which cuts to the heart of its origin and purpose.

When the early Christians understood this reconfiguration of proper worship, it led them to two radical departures from their existing ways of worship as Israelites. First, instead of temple sacrifices, the Eucharistic meal, which commemorates Christ's sacrifice on the cross, would be the center of Christian worship. And second, the day of worship would move from Saturday to the first day of the week — the "Lord's Day," the day of the Resurrection. Writing in the middle of the second century, St. Justin Martyr explains:

> But Sunday is the day on which we all hold our common assembly, because it is the first day on which God, having wrought a change in the darkness and matter, made the world; and Jesus Christ our Saviour on the same day rose from the dead. For He was crucified on the day before that of Saturn [Saturday]; and on the day after that of Saturn, which is the day of the Sun, having appeared to His apostles and disciples, He taught them these things, which we have submitted to you also for your consideration.
>
> — *First Apology*, Chapter 67[13]

While the original institution of the Sabbath goes all the way back to creation itself, the Church Fathers realized that Christ's resurrection inaugurated a new creation which reordered all aspects of the fallen world.

This belief in a new creation is reflected in the term the Fathers often used for Sunday: the "eighth day." The first seven days are a figure of time, but the eighth day is a symbol of eternity: it is the unending day that Christ has brought about by his victory over death. Church Father St. Basil writes:

> The day of the Lord . . . without evening, without succession, and without end is not unknown to Scripture, and it is the day that the Psalmist calls the eighth day, because it is outside this time of weeks. Thus whether you call it day, or whether you call it eternity, you express the same idea.
>
> — *The Hexaemeron*[14]

In a mystical sense, Sunday is a day "outside of time." Participation at Sunday Mass, then, unites the believer to that never-ending day that lies in eternity, the day when Christ reigns over all — a time that will ultimately be consummated with the Lord's second coming.

The connection between Sunday worship and the Lord's final coming is deep and ancient. Christians have historically configured their churches so that they face east when they worship, because it is believed that Christ will return in the east, and they wished to be found ready on that glorious day. The liturgy is full of expectation and hope that the Lord will soon return — "Christ has died, Christ is risen, Christ will come again" — "We proclaim your death, Lord Jesus, until you come in glory." And the day set aside to worship is no longer Saturday, the end of the original creation cycle, but Sunday, the eighth day — outside the old creation and the first and only day of the new eternal creation.

St. Paul writes:

> Therefore let no one pass judgment on you in questions of food and drink or with regard to a festival or a new moon or a sabbath. These are only a shadow of what is to come; but the substance belongs to Christ.

> — Col 2:16-17

The original Sabbath is but a shadow of the true worship made available to us now through the resurrection of Christ. By participating in the Eucharistic worship of Sunday and keeping the day holy through rest and service to others, we proclaim his Lordship and the right ordering of all his gifts of creation. Yet even Sunday worship is but a shadow of the final endless day when all will worship and glorify him unceasingly in heaven. On that "day," we will find eternal rest worshipping the Lord of the Sabbath.

REFERENCES
Mt 12:8

For Reflection
- Has technology become a "lord" of my life?
- Have I set aside daily peaceful time to hear the voice of God?
- How is Sunday different for me than other days? Is it truly set aside for worship and rest?

King of Israel

"He is the King of Israel; let him come down now
from the cross, and we will believe in him."

An ancient Roman image called the *Alexamenos graffito*, dating
to the second century, depicts a man with a donkey's head being
crucified. Another man is present, raising his hand, apparently
worshipping the crucified one. The inscription below the image
says, "Alexamenos worships his God!" It is clearly intended to be
a mockery of the Christian religion. After all, what religion would
worship a condemned criminal? To the average Roman, such a
belief system was unheard of. Their gods may have acted at times
in highly irregular ways, but never would Romans have accepted
as a god a fool of a man who had been condemned by one of their
own governors. The very fact of Jesus' criminal condemnation is
enough to prove that he was not only not a god, but was a failure as
a person as well — surely not worthy of admiration, to say nothing
of worship.

As St. Paul tells us, the image of Christ crucified is "a
stumbling block to Jews and folly to Gentiles" (1 Cor 1:23). The
cross has always been at the heart of the Christian message, but
it has also always been a scandal to the world, even to some of
those who confess Christ. In his Gospel, though, Matthew does
not shrink from detailing the utter humiliation and rejection that
Christ endured, recounting the revilement he received from the
Roman guards, the crowds, the chief priests, and even from both
the thieves who were crucified with him (Mt 27:1-50). He shows
Christ completely abandoned, utterly alone on the cross.

The chief priests are particularly malicious in their rejection of him. To the Gentile onlookers, Jesus is just a pitiful excuse for a revolutionary. His type is all too common, easily mocked, and not taken seriously. But to the chief priests, he is deeply embarrassing: here is a man claiming to be an envoy of their God, yet by his crucifixion he has been proven to be a fake and an impostor. While Jesus hangs on the cross, they mock him:

> "He saved others; he cannot save himself. He is the King of Israel; let him come down now from the cross, and we will believe in him. He trusts in God; let God deliver him now, if he desires him; for he said, 'I am the Son of God.'"
>
> — Mt 27:42-43

Unlike the Gentile people, who address Jesus directly, the chief priests don't even consider him worthy of direct interaction; instead, they speak of him in the third person.

Their mockery revolves around what they feel is one of the most inexcusable claims made about Jesus of Nazareth: "He is the King of Israel." They know that no true King of Israel would allow himself to be so humiliatingly defeated. What victories has he won? Whom has he defeated in battle? "Saul has slain his thousands, and David his ten thousands" (1 Sam 29:5) — but what has Jesus of Nazareth done? Their idea of an authentic Hebrew leader is more along the lines of the Maccabbean rulers, who were able to score at least a few victories over the Seleucids before their dynasty was defeated. God surely would not allow a genuine leader of his Chosen People to die an ignoble death. This is why they challenge him to come down from the cross miraculously. If God were truly behind him, he would deliver Jesus from his enemies, especially in his most dire hour of need. God delivers his favored ones from harm; had he not saved David from the clutches of his foes? And God abandons to their enemies those who do not follow him; had not the destruction of Saul proven that he was God's favored one no longer?

One of the paradoxes of the Christian faith is that it is precisely in the humiliating cross that victory over sin and death is achieved. We can examine this paradox by contemplating one of the ancient psalms of the people of Israel, Psalm 22, the psalm underlying Matthew's account of the crucifixion. Only once does Christ speak from the cross in Matthew's Gospel, and it is to cry out the opening words of this psalm:

> And about the ninth hour Jesus cried with a loud voice, "*Eli, Eli, lama sabachthani?*" that is, "My God, my God, why hast thou forsaken me?"
>
> — Mt 27:46

The entire psalm becomes the backdrop for Matthew's unfolding of the crucifixion of Jesus. The lament of the psalmist — "All who see me mock at me, they make mouths at me, they wag their heads; 'He committed his cause to the LORD; let him deliver him, let him rescue him, for he delights in him!'" (Ps 22:7-8) — echoes in the mocking of the chief priests: "He trusts in God; let God deliver him now" (Mt 27:43). The psalmist's cry, "My tongue cleaves to my jaws" (verse 15), reflects an aspect of the physical suffering of Christ on the cross: "They offered him wine to drink, mingled with gall; but when he tasted it, he would not drink it" (Mt 27:34). Verse 18 of the psalm laments, "They divide my garments among them, and for my raiment they cast lots," which describes exactly what happens to Christ's garment (Mt 27:35). The most sublime connection is to be found in verse 16 of David's psalm: "They have pierced my hands and feet," thus describing, centuries before it occurs, the suffering of Jesus Christ.

Christ in his crucifixion lives out the abominations of Psalm 22, summing them up in his suffering and death on Good Friday. He has willingly chosen to be brought to the very depths of human misery in order to bring us out of it to restoration with God. Even throughout his anguish, Christ's trust in the Father does not waver.

Psalm 22 declares:

> In thee our fathers trusted;
>> they trusted, and thou didst deliver them.
> To thee they cried, and were saved;
>> in thee they trusted, and were not disappointed.
>
> — vv. 4-5

This reflects the trusting outlook of Christ toward his heavenly Father. Christ can hope, even in his agony, because he knows that through his actions all will be reconciled to the Father:

> All the ends of the earth shall remember and turn to the
>> LORD;
>> and all the families of the nations
>>> shall worship before him.
> For dominion belongs to the LORD,
>> and he rules over the nations.
> Yea, to him shall all the proud of the earth bow down;
> before him shall bow all who go down to the dust,
>> and he who cannot keep himself alive.
> Posterity shall serve him;
>> men shall tell of the Lord to the coming generation,
> and proclaim his deliverance to a people yet unborn,
>> that he has wrought it.
>
> — Ps 22:27-31

Herein lies the Christian response to the problem of suffering in the world. Christianity is not Stoicism, embracing pain as something to be endured to strengthen us and detach us from this world — but without other value. No, suffering is redemptive when it is united with Christ's suffering. By suffering and experiencing the pain that comes with living in this fallen world, we are united to Christ on the cross; through this experience, our dependence on the Father is deepened. The Lord did not come to remove suffering and pain but to experience it with us, to make it an offering to the Father, and to allow it to become for us a means of unity with God.

When man brought pain and death to this world with the Fall, then, God did not abandon us to it but made it the very path to holiness. The saints witness to this truth most clearly; suffering is the path freely accepted by all those who most love the Lord. The saints recognize that it is impossible to live in this world without suffering, so instead of trying to minimize it or avoid it, they embrace it as a path of deeper intimacy with the crucified Christ, thereby transforming it into a means of salvation for themselves and others. St. Paul, the apostle of suffering, writes:

> Now I rejoice in my sufferings for your sake, and in my flesh I complete what is lacking in Christ's afflictions for the sake of his body, that is, the church.
>
> — Col 1:24

Christ's path to glorification went through the cross, making it the honored path for any who would follow him.

It is through the cross that Christ is able to bring about a restoration of humanity's fellowship with God — something desired by the chief priests as much as anyone. But the chief priests wanted salvation without repentance, glorification without humility. Unfortunately, we, too, can be the spiritual descendants of the chief priests, seeking the victory of the cross while shirking its cost. While giving lip service to the value of suffering, we often resist it when it comes in an unwelcome form, such as a serious disease, the death of a loved one, or a financial crisis. In resisting these crosses, we want the blessings of Christianity without the suffering and sacrifice that comes with following the crucified one. This is an untenable position. German theologian and martyr Dietrich Bonhoeffer wrote:

> Suffering then is the badge of true discipleship. The disciple is not above his master . . . If we refuse to take up our cross

and submit to suffering and rejection at the hands of men, we forfeit our fellowship with Christ and have ceased to follow him. But if we lose our lives in His service and carry our cross, we shall find our lives again in the fellowship of the cross with Christ.

— *The Cost of Discipleship*[15]

One cannot read Matthew's (or any) Gospel without seeing the centrality of the cross in the life of Christ. And Jesus makes it clear that his followers will share the cross:

"If any man would come after me, let him deny himself and take up his cross and follow me. For whoever would save his life will lose it, and whoever loses his life for my sake will find it."

— Mt 16:24-25

The ultimate fulfillment of Christ's statement is found, of course, in the stories of the martyrs. Giving their lives in witness to the Gospel, they scorned the allurement of this world in order to be faithful to their beloved Lord Jesus Christ.

St. Polycarp, bishop of Smyrna and disciple of St. John the Apostle, was a stalwart defender of the Christian religion and had no desire to be praised by the wise of the world; when the heretic Marcion asked Polycarp if he recognized who he was, the bishop responded, "Yes, indeed, I recognize the firstborn of Satan." At the end of his long life, he was put before a Roman proconsul, who demanded that Polycarp deny Christ and "swear by the genius of Caesar" in order to save his life. The bureaucrat urged Polycarp to "have respect for his age." To this, the saint responded, "Eighty and six years I have been his servant, and he has done me no wrong. How can I then blaspheme my King who saved me?" (*Martyrdom of Polycarp* 9:6, 13).[16] The respect of this world meant nothing to Polycarp, compared with the glories of Christ.

The martyrs of the ancient Church, and all those who have followed them down through the centuries, didn't give their lives out of a sense of duty or valor; they gave them out of love. Their love for Christ was so deep that even suffering and death could not shake it. They knew that by embracing their cross, they would be raised again in union with the resurrected Lord.

This is the scandal of the cross — how can death be victory? How can suffering lead to joy? The chief priests claimed that they would believe in Jesus if he would just come down off that scandalous cross. But St. Jerome questions their sincerity:

> "Let him come down from the cross, and we will believe in him." What a deceitful promise! Which is greater: to come down from the cross while still alive or to rise from the tomb while dead? He rose, and you do not believe. Therefore, even if he came down from the cross, you would not believe.
>
> — *Commentary on Matthew* 4.27.42[17]

Jesus did something even greater than coming down from the cross — he turned the cross, an instrument of death, into the instrument that would defeat death once and for all. Christ, through his cross, is a King infinitely more victorious than Saul or David ever was. He did not defeat the armies of foreign powers; he defeated the power of death, which ruled with an iron fist over the human race. Christ now sings David's hymn of victory against the forces of death:

> I pursued my enemies and destroyed them,
>> and did not turn back until they were consumed.
> I consumed them; I thrust them through, so that they did not rise;
>> they fell under my feet.
> For thou didst gird me with strength for the battle;
>> thou didst make my assailants sink under me.
> Thou didst make my enemies turn their backs to me,
>> those who hated me, and I destroyed them.
>
> — 2 Sam 22:38-41

The cross has become our King's banner of victory, the sign in which we conquer humanity's greatest enemy. Followers of Christ will not be ashamed of the cross, recognizing that the Lord overcame man's enemies not by rejecting the cross but by embracing it. This is the path to resurrection and glorification for Christ and his followers. The chief priests mocked the suffering Christ as a would-be "King of Israel," but through that very suffering, he became the true King of the chosen people. Subjects of this King must seek to live as he did, following the will of the Father no matter where it leads.

REFERENCES
Mt 27:42

For Reflection
- How do I respond when suffering, great or small, arises in my life?
- Do I see my sufferings as a gift from God, a way to draw closer to him?
- How can I begin more fully to unite my sufferings with Christ's?

Teacher

"Teacher, we want to see a miraculous sign from you."

In classic writings, the image of the teacher is a powerful one, although not without a touch of literary schizophrenia. On one hand, teachers are wise sages who guide the protagonist to the resolution of difficult problems. Dostoyevsky's Zosima, for instance, is the central figure passing on a religious vision of love and forgiveness to the young Alexei Karamazov. On the other hand, teachers can be despotic figures who abuse their power and must be overcome by the forces of good. Picture the exquisitely named Wackford Squeers, the sadistic teacher in Dickens' *Nicholas Nickleby*. Regardless of the archetype, however, a teacher exerts tremendous influence — a fact most readers instinctively understand.

Just as "teacher" evokes two disparate images in classic literature, the word is used of Jesus in Matthew's Gospel in two quite dissimilar ways. In preparing for the Last Supper, Jesus tells his disciples:

> "Go into the city to such a one, and say to him, 'The Teacher says, My time is at hand; I will keep the passover at your house with my disciples.'"
>
> — Mt 26:18

Here at the end of his life, in the hours leading up to the salvific events of Holy Thursday and Good Friday, Jesus identifies himself simply as "the Teacher." To this unnamed disciple in the city, the title "Teacher" refers with certainty to Jesus of Nazareth. Why does

Christ use this title at this time? Perhaps it is because teaching has been his primary task before the events of Holy Week.

If Jesus had done nothing else in his life after this point, he might have gone down in history as a great Jewish teacher, leading a great reform of the Jewish people and teaching them a new way of life under the Law. Matthew himself presents Christ as the exalted teacher of a new Covenant: Christ's Sermon on the Mount in Chapters 5-7, as well as his series of parables in Chapter 13, evoke the image of a teacher enlightening his pupils on a new and better way of life. As the Passion had not yet occurred, many outside Jesus' "inner circle" knew him as simply a teacher.

However, the public image of Jesus as teacher was two-sided. In every case save one in which someone else addresses Jesus as "teacher" in Matthew's Gospel, that person is accusing, challenging, or testing him. The term — one of great respect in the Jewish culture of the day — becomes derisive in the mouths of Christ's opponents. Clearly, they see him as a false teacher whose influence over the people must be resisted.

Jesus' primary Jewish enemies — the Pharisees and the Sadducees — both adopt this scornful attitude. During Holy Week, the effort to "entangle [Jesus] in his talk" (Mt 22:15) intensifies. First, the Pharisees use the hated subject of the Romans as a weapon against Jesus, asking:

> "Teacher, we know that you are true, and teach the way of God truthfully, and care for no man; for you do not regard the position of men. Tell us, then, what you think. Is it lawful to pay taxes to Caesar, or not?"
>
> — Mt 22:16-17

Every teacher who has ever had a know-it-all student recognizes the tone used here. The Pharisees first seek to soften Jesus up with flattery, then to pounce on him when he teaches error. Contrary to their complimentary tone, they hope that any answer Jesus gives will condemn him. If he says, "Pay the tax," the Jewish people will no longer look to him as a possible Messiah, for gaining independence for Israel from foreign oppressors was seen as a primary duty of the Anointed One. However, if he advocates refusing to pay, then the Roman authorities will surely move against him. Either way, the Pharisees will rid themselves of this rabble-rouser. Thus, their use of the term "teacher" is rich in irony: they have no desire to learn, and lack the humility all students need in order to do so.

But Jesus is the great reader of human hearts. Although he is rich in mercy and compassion, he has no patience for those who openly mock the things of God. He responds first by exposing their inner thoughts: "Why put me to the test, you hypocrites?" (Mt 22:18). By doing this, he reveals to all present the falseness of his inquirers. Then, for the sake of the crowd, he brilliantly gives his now-famous answer:

> "Show me the money for the tax." And they brought him a coin. And Jesus said to them, "Whose likeness and inscription is this?" They said, "Caesar's." Then he said to them, "Render therefore to Caesar the things that are Caesar's, and to God the things that are God's."
>
> — Mt 22:19-21

Most who have read this passage naturally focus on its teaching regarding the duties of the Christian to the state. However, Christ's words here should not be limited to a simple lesson in civics; he is succinctly putting all things in their proper order. A mere coin that is created by Caesar properly belongs to Caesar — he has the right to ask for it back. But what belongs to God? The human heart. And God has the right to ask for man to give it back to him. The Pharisees have corrupted their hearts by not giving them back to God. Thus, Jesus turns their question about a minor political issue into an opportunity to teach his hearers what is truly essential — giving one's whole heart in service to God.

Next, the Sadducees take up where the Pharisees left off (Mt 22:23-33). Unlike the Pharisees, they aim to ensnare him with a theological rather than a political question, inquiring about the heavenly status of a woman married seven times. Like the Pharisees, they address Jesus as "teacher," even though their hearts are too hardened to learn from him. Like the Pharisees, they intend to trap Jesus in order to condemn him. Instead, they receive condemnation when Jesus says, "You know neither the scriptures nor the power of God," (Mt 22:29) and exposes the fallacy of their proposition. The Sadducees, by denying the belief in the resurrection of the dead, are single-minded in their focus on this world and its realities, never considering anything beyond it. But Jesus is single-minded in his focus on his heavenly Father, and so uses this trap as an opportunity to educate his listeners on heavenly realities. Even the joys of marriage, which Christ highly exalts, are nothing compared to the joy of everlasting union with God in heaven.

Again, Jesus turns a minor question — this time of religious law — into an opportunity to teach about what is essential in human existence. Unfortunately, the Sadducees' underlying mentality is the same as that of the Pharisees: Christ's explanation is like seeds falling on rocky ground. They do not have "ears to hear" (Mt 13:9) and refuse to turn their hearts toward him.

The Lord recognizes the core reason why people reject his teachings. It is not due to lack of intelligence or learning, but pride and hardness of heart. Quoting from the prophet Isaiah, he acknowledges:

> "'You shall indeed hear but never understand,
> and you shall indeed see but never perceive.
> For this people's heart has grown dull,
> and their ears are heavy of hearing,
> and their eyes they have closed,
> lest they should perceive with their eyes,

and hear with their ears,
and understand with their heart,
and turn for me to heal them.'"

— Mt 13:14-15

The pride of Jesus' enemies is the stumbling block to knowledge of God and his ways. Yet Jesus uses their attacks to teach those in the crowd who *are* open to learning. Matthew states that those around Jesus "marveled" and were "astonished" by his teaching. Here was a true teacher of Israel.

This calls to mind Luke's account of the boy Jesus in the temple, teaching the scholars and leaving them, too, astonished by his answers (Lk 2:46-47). Thus, although both the Pharisees and Sadducees called him "teacher" without actually accepting him as one, Jesus used their questions as opportunities to reveal his message to those willing to learn.

When we come to the account of Jesus being addressed as "teacher" by the rich young man (Mt 19:16-22), we find an episode most illuminative of one who actually looked to Jesus as a teacher in the ways of God. It begins simply enough: "And behold, one came up to him, saying, 'Teacher, what good deed must I do, to have eternal life?'" It appears that this is a man who recognizes and desires knowledge in the important things in life. Being rich, he has access to all that this world can offer but senses that these material benefits cannot fully satisfy him. He desires to learn what he can, and instinctively recognizes that Jesus may be one who can show him a better way.

Anyone familiar with the teachings of Christianity might be surprised by Christ's initial response. It does not speak of grace or sacraments or faith. It is instead a somewhat pedestrian answer that any Jewish teacher of the time might have given: "If you would enter life, keep the commandments." This response the rich young man understands, as he inquires further, "Which [ones]?" Again, Jesus' reply does not leave the boundaries of traditional Judaism:

"You shall not kill, You shall not commit adultery, You shall not steal, You shall not bear false witness, Honor your father and mother, and, You shall love your neighbor as yourself."

Prior to this moment, the rich young man has seen Jesus as merely a teacher, and Jesus has done nothing to disabuse him of that notion. Jesus is testing him in order to determine how deeply he desires this "eternal life."

And there does seem to be hope: the young man is not satisfied with these standard answers. Surely, he has heard these responses before, and he recognizes that they are not sufficient. We can guess that Jesus is not the first teacher to whom he has addressed these questions. So he persists, "All these I have observed; what do I still lack?" Experience has shown him that the Mosaic Law is not an end in itself, but instead points to something greater.

Now, Jesus leaves his role as a Jewish teacher and reveals that the fulfillment of all this man's desires, the fulfillment of the Mosaic Law, is standing right in front of him. "If you would be perfect, go, sell what you possess and give to the poor, and you will have treasure in heaven; and come, follow me." Jesus is telling him: "Don't look to me as just a teacher, acknowledge me as your Lord! Give your entire life to my service! Only then can you be completely fulfilled." It is by making the person of Jesus the central part of his life that this man can be satisfied.

Israel had always looked to the Law as the means for drawing closer to God, but Jesus is changing this proposition radically. The Law, with its emphasis on the failure of man to "be holy" (cf. Lev 11:44), points to the need for a savior, and Jesus is that figure. Now, he will be the means by which one draws into union with the eternal God. But there is a price: the disciple must give up everything and give Christ dominion in his life. As Dietrich Bonhoeffer reminded the world, grace is most assuredly not cheap. It cost Jesus his life, and he asks his followers to give up theirs in return. Jesus is offering the rich young man eternal life, but at the cost of his earthly life.

Three centuries later, the demand of Jesus in this very passage would lead another rich young man, St. Anthony, to give away all his possessions and withdraw completely from the world in a life of strict asceticism, becoming the founder of monasticism and setting an example that changed millions of lives. However, this biblical account doesn't have such a happy ending. The rich young man, unwilling to see Jesus as anything more than just a human teacher, "went away sorrowful; for he had great possessions." He is content to be a student but unwilling to be a disciple. He wanted a philosophy to live by, but Christ shows him a faith to die for. He might be able to accept the worth of the great Jewish moral code, and even understand the value of following it, but when Jesus asks him to give up his possessions and be completely devoted to him, he finds the attachments of this world too powerful. Although he knows that they cannot completely fulfill him, he is averse to taking the risk of life without them. It was not simply learning, it was *faith*: faith that life with Jesus and acceptance of the Gospel path would be the realization of all his desires.

There is much we can learn from Jesus, but this knowledge is only salvific and completely fulfilling when our hearts are open to the *person* of Christ. Only then may we be taught the means — and given the ability — to gain "eternal life."

REFERENCES

Mt 8:19, 9:11, 10:24-25, 12:38, 17:24, 19:16, 22:16, 22:24, 22:36, 26:18

For Reflection

- Are the teachings of Jesus integrated into every aspect of my life?
- Do I conform myself to his way of life or the ways of the world?
- Do I allow Jesus to be not just my teacher, but also my Lord?

Christon

"You are the Christ . . . "

The Eastern Church has a delightful tradition of transforming the names of certain beloved saints by adding a title to them. Thus, St. Simeon is "Righteous Simeon the God-receiver," St. Gregory of Nazianzus is "Gregory the Theologian," and St. Maximus becomes "St. Maximus the Confessor." By altering these holy men's names, the Church wants to reflect upon the deep reality of their contribution to the cause of Christ. Of course, Jesus himself initiates this practice when he decides to rename his impetuous disciple, Simon, "Peter" — or "rock" — and says that the very Church would be built on him (cf. Mt 16:18).

Jesus himself also has a title bestowed upon him by his followers: *Christ*. Adding to Jesus' name the title Christ, which means "anointed one," becomes commonplace within the Church almost immediately after his ascension; Paul's letters, only twenty years later, use the title without explanation. The first definitive doctrinal statement on the person of Christ — the Nicene Creed — shows that this practice was established as the standard of the Church when it professes, "We believe in one Lord, Jesus Christ." Devotionally, too, the title became part of the name of Jesus. The Jesus Prayer, one of the most popular prayers recited over the centuries, states simply, "Lord Jesus Christ, have mercy on me, a sinner." To most Christians (and even non-Christians), the title "Christ" has, for practical purposes, become the surname of Jesus of Nazareth.

But the title *Christ* has deep meaning and far-reaching

consequences. Above all, it signifies that Jesus is the fulfillment of promises reaching back to the beginning of time itself. He is the long-awaited "anointed one," the one prophesied from ages past, beginning with the promise found in the *protoevangelium* of Genesis 3:15, when God told the enemy of mankind:

> "I will put enmity between you and the woman,
>   and between your seed and her seed;
> he shall bruise your head,
>   and you shall bruise his heel."

There will come one, born of a woman, who will not succumb to the devil's temptations. He will defeat the forces of sin and death in the end and bring salvation to the world. Christ is thus the "new Adam": as the first Adam brought sin and death into the world by yielding to the devil's temptations, so Christ brings grace and life by his defeat of the devil.

> If, because of one man's trespass, death reigned through that one man, much more will those who receive the abundance of grace and the free gift of righteousness reign in life through the one man Jesus Christ.
>
> — Rom 5:17

The mission of the Christ is first and foremost to reverse the damage done to the human race by Adam.

The title Christ also represents the triple-office the new Adam would employ to defeat sin and death: priest, prophet, and king. In the Old Testament, each person holding one of these offices — representing God's appointed leaders over his people — was anointed in some fashion. Elijah anointed Elisha as a prophet by throwing his mantle over Elisha (1 Kings 19:16-19). The high priest's head was anointed with oil (Ex 29:1-9) — as was the king's, as we see with Saul, David, and Solomon (1 Sam 10:1, 2 Sam 2:4, 1 Kings 1:34). The Christ, however, would be the anointed one *par excellence.* his anointing would come from God above; and, at the baptism of Jesus, the Spirit of God anoints him as the Father proclaims, "This is my beloved Son, with whom I am well pleased" (Mt 3:17). In his person he fulfills all three old covenant roles, and in these roles overcomes the power of sin and death that rules humanity. As priest, he offers himself as sacrifice to the Father, a spotless lamb who takes away the sins of the world. As prophet, he proclaims the wisdom of God, pointing out the way to everlasting life. And as king, he rules over all, even death:

> Then comes the end, when he delivers the kingdom to God the Father after destroying every rule and every authority and power. For he must reign until he has put all his enemies under his feet. The last enemy to be destroyed is death.
>
> — 1 Cor 15:24-26

All the kings, priests, and prophets of the Old Testament are but shadows of the reality that is the true anointed one: Jesus Christ. Even the great role models of ancient days like Elisha, David, and Aaron were unable to overcome that most pernicious of human problems — sin and death.

The Jewish people, realizing their inability to overcome these fundamental problems, put their hope in the One who one day would be triumphant. This one word — hope — sums up the Jewish expectation of the Christ.

Throughout all her history, Israel had been more often defeated than victorious. Whether it was the Babylonians or the Romans, Israel had been unable to overcome her enemies. Even when Israel tasted brief success — during the reign of Solomon, for instance — her unfaithfulness to the Lord had led to disaster. But through all of that history, the faithful had at least the hope of the future Christ, who would exalt God's people above all nations and restore the covenant with God.

Hope is one of the most powerful forces in human existence. Without hope, it's almost impossible to accept the hardships of life and overcome even the smallest of obstacles; with it, the fate of entire nations can change. The Church has defined hope as one of the "theological" virtues, along with faith and love, because hope's ultimate object is God. Hope is always directed toward a better future, and man's ultimate future of true happiness is union with God himself. This is a primary reason why Jesus was misunderstood and rejected by many of his co-religionists: their hopes were directed toward an earthly resolution, but the mission of Christ was to fulfill the greatest hope of all, fellowship with God.

Of course, Satan, that instigator of our first father's Fall, does not allow the Christ to restore the world to fellowship with God without a fight. Matthew highlights the enmity between Jesus and Satan by recounting Christ's temptations in the desert before he commences his public ministry (Mt 4:1-11). We can see that these temptations hearken back to Adam's temptation in the Garden when Satan challenges Jesus, "If you are the Son of God." Satan wants to know if this "Son of God" will act any differently than the first "son of God," Adam. Clearly, intrinsic to Christ's mission is a battle against the "spiritual hosts of wickedness in the heavenly places" (Eph 6:12) that are pitted against man.

Unfortunately, belief in the existence of this battle, even the existence of its participants, is treated today as an embarrassing relic of a long-gone culture. Surely there is not *really* a purely evil supernatural being that "prowls around like a roaring lion, seeking some one to devour" (1 Pet 5:8). Modern man, we're told, has outgrown such fairytales and superstitions. The Scriptures, however, display no such embarrassment about the existence of Satan. He is always there in the story of salvation history, literally from Genesis to Revelation. He was directly involved in man's original Fall, and Christ clearly sees the defeat of Satan as part of the drama of man's restoration and glorification. The great victory of Satan in modern times has been to convince the world to ignore him.

Jesus was not so gullible. He knew that the role of the Christ was to overthrow the devil's dominion and to defeat that child of the devil, death. A life in imitation of Christ will likewise lead his followers into battle with Satan and his fallen angels. In the center of this cosmic battle between good and evil stands the Christ; it is he who will be the one to overcome evil and establish the reign of God.

The evangelist Matthew realizes this; one of his goals in writing his Gospel is to show his primarily Jewish readers that Jesus is the one who was promised, over and over, since the dawn of man. He begins by showing that this Jesus of Nazareth is qualified to be the fulfillment of the promises of a Christ, giving a number of proofs in this regard in the first two chapters of his Gospel. First, he recounts the familial pedigree that supports Jesus as Christ, by reciting the "genealogy of Jesus Christ, the son of David, the son of Abraham" (Mt 1:1). He knows that a Jewish reader will not even consider as the Christ one who is not a child of Israel and a son of David. Joseph's adoption of Jesus as his son, detailed by Matthew as well, makes him a part of the Davidic line. Because many knew that Jesus hailed from Nazareth, Matthew points out that his birthplace is actually the same as the birthplace of the promised Christ, giving yet another proof. Matthew also gives other demonstrations, such as Jesus having to flee to Egypt and then return, consequently fulfilling the prophecy that "out of Egypt I will call my son" (Mt 2:15). The theme of Matthew's Gospel is thus established: Jesus of Nazareth, born in Bethlehem of Mary and adopted by Joseph, is the long-awaited Christ.

But then, something curious happens. After this clear declaration of Jesus as the Christ in his opening chapters, Matthew allows this question to fade into the background as Jesus goes about his work, preaching and healing. The possible identification of Jesus as the Christ does not again come to the forefront until his trial, when the high priest demands, "I adjure you by the living God, tell us if you are the Christ, the Son of God" (Mt 26:63). In this, we see Matthew's brilliance as a storyteller. He does not clumsily hammer home that Jesus is the Christ; instead, after placing the possibility in his reader's mind, he allows him to live out the doubt, even defiance, of those who encountered Jesus as he performed his public ministry. As the people surrounding Jesus seek to know if he is the Christ, the reader, too, is drawn into this central question, looking for any evidence that Jesus is indeed the promised one.

Matthew shows that Jesus did nothing to publicly proclaim himself as Christ. Jesus knew that many Jews misunderstood the true meaning behind the prophecies, that the Christ was to free them not from political oppression but the oppression of sin. Instead of confronting this misperception directly, he gently leads people to the truth, with the aid of the Holy Spirit. We see this in the one instance in Matthew in which someone declares openly that Jesus is the Christ: Peter's confession of faith (Mt 16:16).

Jesus asks his apostles the question that has reverberated through the centuries, "Who do men say that the Son of Man is?" The apostles give various answers, but then Jesus goes to the heart of the matter: "Who do *you* say that I am?" Now, the apostles are on the spot: they cannot hide behind the conjectures of the crowds. They must confess what they believe about Jesus. And underlying this question is another one: "Do you think that I am the long-promised Christ, foretold in the Scriptures since the beginning of time?" Jesus doesn't proclaim his status as Christ to them. Instead, he wants to see if his closest followers have been open to the prompting of the Holy Spirit. And in response, Simon Peter boldly proclaims, "You are the Christ, the Son of the living God."

The careful reader will note that Peter's confession actually consists of *two* confessions: Jesus is the "Christ," and he is the "Son of the living God." These two titles, although interrelated, are distinct. The first title, "Christ," describes what Jesus does, while the second, "Son of the living God," describes who he is. With divine help, Peter recognizes that Jesus is not simply another prophet or teacher, but actually the fulfillment of promises dating back to the Fall (cf. Mt 16:17). Jesus is the one who will defeat the enemy of mankind and will restore Israel and the whole world to communion with God.

Fulton J. Sheen once said that Jesus is the only person ever pre-announced. It is ironic that it took divine revelation for someone to recognize the one person whom God had been promising and describing for so long. The effects of the Fall were great, indeed.

The advent of the Christ, an event awaited for centuries, is the event that Christians boldly proclaim has occurred by way of a poor carpenter from first-century Nazareth in Galilee. Sin and death have now been defeated by this Christ.

> "O death, where is thy victory?
> O death, where is thy sting?"
> . . . But thanks be to God, who gives us the victory through
> our Lord Jesus Christ.
>
> — 1 Cor 15:55, 57

Death is no longer something we must fear, but rather, the passageway to eternal life with Christ. Jesus is the Christ, the anointed one who has overcome the devil and defeated death, the bridge uniting all people to the Father.

REFERENCES

Mt 1:1, 1:16, 1:17, 1:18, 11:2, 16:16, 16:20, 23:10, 26:63, 26:68, 27:17, 27:22

For Reflection

- In my daily life, do I let hope reign?
- What causes me to let go of that hope and fall into fear?
- How is that fear manifested in my thoughts, actions, and words?

Lord

"Lord, save us! We are perishing!" (NAB)

In the embryonic days of the American nation, the founding fathers debated the title to be given to their new leader, George Washington. One title Washington rejected forcefully was "king." The idea of an American royalty was repugnant to General Washington, who believed any sort of privileged class would defy the democratic ideals of the new nation. This country's fundamental ideal that "all men were created equal," while often put in practice imperfectly, has remained embedded in the American psyche: no man or woman is greater than any other.

Ancient cultures lived by quite a different rule. Each person in society belonged to a certain class, with little or no opportunity to change that status. Those above one's station were to be treated with respect, and those below were to be considered there for your service.

In the Greek-speaking Roman Empire, one term — "*kyrios*," translated "Lord" — was used to address anyone of superior status. The term could have a variety of meanings: from the equivalent of the English word "sir" to the title a slave used to address his master or a woman her husband. It was also a term used to address the emperor, and as Caesar-worship developed throughout the Empire, the term "Lord" began to have divine connotations as well. Fundamentally, "Lord" means one "having power," and more specifically, it was used of those who had power over others.

Greek-speaking Jews of the Empire used the term "Lord" as

117

well, often in the same fashion as their Gentile neighbors. But there was one exception. In the Greek translation of the Old Testament, called the Septuagint, the word "Lord" was used in place of the divine name, which was unutterable. No Jew would say the name of God, so "Lord" was used as a substitute for that name. Thus, because they assigned the term "Lord" to the Almighty, Jews would never use it to refer to the emperor.

In the Gospel of Matthew, Jesus is addressed as "Lord" twelve times. Considering that Jesus is a simple carpenter from an obscure town, this usage should immediately raise questions. Over whom does a peasant like Jesus have power? Whom can he command? By the very fact that he is addressed as Lord, we can see that people must have perceived instinctively that he had a power beyond his outward state in life. Never do those who oppose him— the chief priests, Judas, or the Roman authorities — call him this title; it is only the disciples and those who seek him out for aid who call him "Lord." In those instances of someone referring to Jesus as "Lord," the speaker is *asking for something;* he is in a posture of supplication. He believes that Jesus can effect change in his life in some way or other. Chapter 8 of Matthew alone gives three separate instances where this occurs: the man with leprosy, the centurion with a sick servant, and the apostles asking Jesus to save them from the storm.

> "Lord, if you will, you can make me clean." (Mt 8:2)
>
> "Lord, my servant is lying paralyzed at home, in terrible distress." (Mt 8:6)
>
> "Lord, save us! We are perishing!" (Mt 8:25)

The first instance — the healing of the man with leprosy (Mt 8:1-4) — is especially instructive. The leper states simply, "Lord, if you will, you can make me clean." This man has the proper attitude for a prayer of petition; an attitude having two aspects: (1) faith that Jesus does have the power to grant the request ("you *can* make me clean"), and (2) submission to God's will ("if you will"). St. John Chrysostom, commenting on this passage, states:

With great fervor before Jesus' knees, the leper pleaded with him with sincere faith. He discerned who Jesus was. He did not state conditionally, "If you request it of God" or "If you pray for me." Rather, he said simply, "If you will, you can make me clean." He did not pray, "Lord, cleanse me." Rather, he leaves everything to the Lord and makes his own recovery depend entirely on him. Thus he testified that all authority belongs to him.

— Homily on the Gospel of Matthew 25.1 [18]

The leper's request is the model for the proper attitude in prayer: by acknowledging Jesus as Lord, the leper recognizes that he has both the *power* to affect a change, and the *authority* to decide whether to act. It takes a great faith to recognize that the Lord has the power to overcome any difficulty and address any need. The leper had an incurable disease that ostracized him from human contact. He had no reason to believe that it could ever be reversed — yet he did believe.

When we're presented with a particularly daunting challenge, we can hesitate asking for the Lord's intercession. We seem to feel that perhaps it would be better not to ask of the Lord, for fear that he might "fail" us. But Jesus rejects this possibility; he claims all power and authority for himself: "All authority in heaven and on earth has been given to me" (Mt 28:18), he tells his apostles before ascending to his Father. Not only does he have the power and authority necessary, he desires to use it for his followers.

"What man of you, if his son asks him for bread, will give him a stone? Or if he asks for a fish, will give him a serpent? If you then, who are evil, know how to give good gifts to your children, how much more will your Father who is in heaven give good things to those who ask him!"

— Mt 7:9-13

A prayer being "unanswered" is never a sign of a lack of power on the part of the Lord; it is a sign that *the particular answer we desired* was not part of God's will.

Perhaps the most beautiful prayer of supplication is the Jesus Prayer, which rightly starts by addressing Jesus as Lord: "Lord Jesus Christ, have mercy on me, a sinner." This prayer has its roots in the parable of the Pharisee and the tax collector:

> "Two men went up into the temple to pray, one a Pharisee and the other a tax collector. The Pharisee stood and prayed thus with himself, 'God, I thank thee that I am not like other men, extortioners, unjust, adulterers, or even like this tax collector. I fast twice a week, I give tithes of all that I get.' But the tax collector, standing far off, would not even lift up his eyes to heaven, but beat his breast, saying, 'God, be merciful to me a sinner!' I tell you, this man went down to his house justified rather than the other; for every one who exalts himself will be humbled, but he who humbles himself will be exalted."
>
> — Lk 18:10-14

This prayer — beloved especially in the East — comes to Christ with the heart of the tax collector, acknowledging that Christ has power and authority over the most personal of realms: man's sinfulness. No power or authority of this world is able to grant mercy to another for his sins. Yet the cry of the Jesus Prayer recognizes that there is One who has such power and authority: Jesus Christ. Furthermore, this prayer acknowledges the true divide between Jesus and the petitioner: he is "Lord," the supplicant is "a sinner." Only one has power over sin, and it is the great joy of the Christian faith that this one is full of mercy for all who call to him. No matter how desperate the situation, Jesus is waiting to extend his mercy.

This leads to another commonality among those who address Jesus as "Lord" in Matthew's Gospel: a certain desperation in their requests. They are at the end of the line and see no other way to resolve their problems, aside from begging Jesus.

In Matthew 20:30-34, two blind men sitting by the roadside hear that Jesus is coming and immediately begin to cry out in a loud voice, "*Lord*, have mercy on us, Son of David!" They continue to shout, even though the crowd attempts to silence them. Their desperation at their plight is so great — as is their expectation of the ability of Jesus, their Lord, to solve it — that they don't care what others may think or say. They simply throw themselves at his feet and trust in his mercy, believing that he will give what is best for them. Jesus' response? To look upon them "in pity" and to touch them (Mt 20:34).

To those who would only come to him as a means to an end, however, Jesus also doesn't hesitate to give a frightening warning:

> "Not every one who says to me, 'Lord, Lord,' shall enter the kingdom of heaven, but he who does the will of my Father who is in heaven."
>
> — Mt 7:21

Those who receive benefits from others can begin to see their benefactors as simply fulfillers of their personal needs. Christians aren't immune from this tendency — witness preachers who promise earthly gain to those who believe. They assert that Christ will bestow on each person whatever material blessings he asks for: Christ's role in a believer's life, it seems, becomes one of dispensing wealth and possessions.

It may be easy to condemn such behavior, but too often we do the same in our own hearts. Are we willing to accept the Lord's will, even when it is not our will? We can desire something with good intentions, but that desire can become an obstacle in the spiritual life if we become angry or despondent when God does not grant it to us — even an idol, if it is placed at the center of our lives. When God answers the request with "no" or "wait," we lose faith in his loving kindness toward us. In doing so, our will replaces a desire to do the will of the Father.

This is a path that can lead to spiritual harm, even estrangement from our loving Father. Although Christ is the source of all blessings, and we can be confident that we can "ask, and it will be given" (Mt 7:7), Jesus is not a vending machine! Above all our desires must be our desire to do the will of the Father. This is how we acknowledge the Lordship of Christ. The prayer of the leper, again, is instructive: "Lord, if you will, you can make me clean" (Mt 8:2).

While the term "Lord" can be a term of respect toward a superior, when applied to Christ it becomes imbued with its fullest meaning: it is an acknowledgement that Jesus is Lord over both heaven and earth and over realms both spiritual and physical. Paul declares Christ's total lordship in his letter to the Philippians:

> God has highly exalted him and bestowed on him the name which is above every name, that at the name of Jesus every knee should bow, in heaven and on earth and under the earth, and every tongue confess that Jesus Christ is Lord, to the glory of God the Father.
>
> — Phil 2:9-11

For a first-century Roman Jew like Paul, this statement is revolutionary. In the first place, it is a direct challenge to the "lordship" of the emperor: Paul is implying to the inhabitants of the Roman colony Philippi that their true Lord is not Caesar, but Jesus of Nazareth.

This was an assertion that would land any Roman citizen in jail (and, in fact, Paul wrote this letter from prison). But to the Jew, this was even more radical. Remember that the Jews had replaced the divine name of God with the title "LORD" in their Scriptures, for fear of uttering the most holy name of God. This title was infused with divine prerogatives — which, Paul proclaims, have been handed over to Jesus of Nazareth. Paul writes that "every knee should bow . . . and every tongue confess" the Lordship of Christ. He takes this language directly from God's declaration to Isaiah that to him "every knee shall bow, every tongue shall swear" (Is 45:23). This pronouncement of God comes in the most explicitly monotheistic section of the Old Testament (chapters 40-55 of Isaiah), which proclaims the God of Israel to be the only true God and that God's glory cannot be given to anyone else. Yet Paul announces that God has handed over all of his glory to his Son, Jesus Christ, and the mystery of the Trinity begins to unfold. God the Father pours out his entire self into the Son, who is thus eternally begotten as the second person of the Godhead, equal to God in all things. The humble peasant from Galilee, whom no one would rightly acknowledge as "Lord," is the one to whom true lordship is given. He is not only Lord over the false god Caesar, but he is equal in lordship to the one true God of Israel. In light of his glory, the only response can be "Lord Jesus Christ, have mercy on me, a sinner."

REFERENCES

Mt 7:21-22, 8:2, 8:6-8, 8:21, 8:25, 9:28, 14:28-30, 15:22-27, 16:22, 17:4, 17:15, 18:21, 20:30-33, 21:3

For Reflection

- Do I wait on the Lord?
- Do I persevere in prayer?
- Do I let my prayer change me?

Nazarene

What was spoken by the prophets might be
fulfilled, "He shall be called a Nazarene."

Near the end of his Gospel, St. John writes:

> These are written that you may believe that Jesus is the Christ,
> the Son of God, and that believing you may have life in his
> name.
>
> — Jn 20:31

This is the purpose of all the Gospels: to demonstrate the
saving fact that Jesus is the Christ. The opening two chapters of
Matthew's Gospel contain a flurry of apologetic material toward
this purpose, wherein the evangelist focuses on addressing any
arguments against Jesus' credentials as the Christ. He shows that
Jesus is a true son of David through adoption by Joseph; that Jesus
is the one promised by Isaiah in the prophecy, "A virgin shall
conceive and bear a son, and his name shall be called Emmanuel"
(Is 7:14); and that he was born in the city of David, Bethlehem
of Judea. The culmination of Matthew's arguments comes at the
conclusion of Chapter 2:

> But when [Joseph] heard that Archelaus reigned over Judea in
> place of his father Herod, he was afraid to go there, and being
> warned in a dream he withdrew to the district of Galilee. And
> he went and dwelt in a city called Nazareth, that what was
> spoken by the prophets might be fulfilled, "He shall be called
> a Nazarene."
>
> — Mt 2:22-23

A "Nazarene"? Prophecies of virgin births and the town of Bethlehem are familiar to most Christians, but the prediction that the Messiah would be a Nazarene is largely unknown. And for good reason: to the best of our knowledge, no such prophecy exists in the Old Testament or even in extra-canonical Jewish books. In fact, Nazareth was such an obscure village that it is not once mentioned in the Old Testament. Nathaniel demonstrates the typical attitude toward this village in John's Gospel, when he rejects the possibility of the Christ coming from there with a dismissive "Can anything good come out of Nazareth?" (Jn 1:46). The idea of the Christ hailing from Nazareth appears to contradict the royal claim that he would be from the same town as great King David, Bethlehem.

What, then, could Matthew be referring to in this passage? Scripture scholars have long debated this, arriving at no absolute resolution. Perhaps Matthew was quoting a prophetic text known to him and familiar to his readers, though not in our modern Old Testament canon. In that case, the prophecy would be much like the one that proclaims that the Christ will come from Bethlehem (Mic 5:2), simply limiting the pool from which the Messiah will originate. This is unlikely, however, since the village of Nazareth didn't even exist until shortly before Matthew's time.

So Scripture scholars throughout the centuries have struggled to produce other theories as to the meaning of this verse. St. Jerome, for instance, found a spiritual meaning behind the text:

> If this could have been found in the Scriptures, he never would have said, "Because it has been spoken by the prophets," but he would rather have spoken more plainly: "Because it has been spoken by *a* prophet." As it is now, in speaking of prophets in general he has shown that he has not taken the specific words but rather the sense from the Scriptures. "Nazarene" is understood as "holy." Every Scripture attests that the Lord was to be holy.
>
> — *Commentary on Matthew* 1.2.23[19]

Cyril of Alexandria had a similar interpretation:

> But if 'Nazarene' is interpreted to mean "holy" . . . this is the designation found in many instances. For Daniel calls him "holy" or "of the holy ones."

— Fragment 16[20]

The association between "Nazarene" and "holy" most likely originates with "Nazarene" being transcribed as "Nazoree," a term that denotes membership in a sect (such as the Pharisees or the Sadducees). Members of sects are "set apart" from the world, which is also a meaning of "holy" — being set apart from the profane world in some fashion. Some biblical scholars have therefore seen this prophecy merely as a statement of Christ's holiness.

Jerome and Cyril also acknowledged another possible meaning. Perhaps Matthew was associating the term "Nazarene" with the Hebrew word *nezer,* which means "branch." This would then refer to the prophecy in Isaiah 11:1:

> There shall come forth a shoot from the stump of Jesse, and a *branch* shall grow out of his roots.

Matthew may simply be establishing that Jesus is from the root of Jesse, one of his branches. This is one of the most common interpretations of this prophecy; in fact, in the RSV translation of the Bible, you see a reference to Isaiah 11:1 linked with Matthew 2:23.

Consider, also, the first-century usage of the term "Nazarene." We find an example of it in Acts 24:5, when leaders of the Jews are accusing Paul before the governor:

> "For we have found this man a pestilent fellow, an agitator among all the Jews throughout the world, and a ringleader of the sect of the Nazarenes."

So "Nazarene" was used in a derisive fashion against the Christians. Most Jews, especially those in Jerusalem, looked down on the inhabitants of Galilee — particularly those from such a town as Nazareth. At the time of Christ, the village of Nazareth had no more than 500 inhabitants and was inconsequential in every regard. Romans, needless to say, would have been even more contemptuous of such an insignificant origin. (In many ways, their attitude was similar to that of a modern New Yorker toward a small southern town.) The people of Galilee even had a distinctive accent that set them further apart from their more cosmopolitan neighbors. Thus, associating the Christians with such a town was denigrating them. Who need take them seriously?

Matthew, however, turns this mocking term of derision into a badge of honor, proclaiming that such a humble association is in keeping with the prophets' conception of the Messiah. He would be of humble origins, they had announced, mocked and mistreated by those in power (cf. Is 53, Ps 22). Matthew is preparing his readers for the first beatitude of Jesus, "Blessed are the poor in spirit, for theirs is the kingdom of heaven" (Mt 5:3). Those looking for a Messiah should not look to the great and mighty of this world, but instead to a humble carpenter from an obscure town. This is a mystery hidden from all except those who are poor in spirit as well.

Poverty of spirit takes us deep into the heart of God. The Scriptures detail God's love for the poor and his desire to lift them up. Many psalms sing of God answering the cry of the poor against the rich and powerful, and many of the heroes of the Old and New Testaments have humble origins. But the greatest example of God lifting up one who is poor is found in another Nazarene, the Virgin Mary. God raises a humble Galilean peasant girl to be the very Mother of God. Of all the great women in history God could have chosen, he desired this small-town girl to be the instrument through which his Word entered the world. Mary herself proclaims this most beautifully in the *Magnificat*:

"My soul magnifies the Lord, and my spirit rejoices in
    God my Savior,

for he has regarded the low estate of his handmaiden.

For behold, henceforth all generations will call me blessed;

for he who is mighty has done great things for me,

and holy is his name.

And his mercy is on those who fear him from generation
to generation

He has shown strength with his arm,

he has scattered the proud in the imagination of their
    hearts,

he has put down the mighty from their thrones,

and exalted those of low degree;

he has filled the hungry with good things,

and the rich he has sent empty away.

He has helped his servant Israel,

in remembrance of his mercy,

as he spoke to our fathers,

to Abraham and to his posterity for ever."

— Lk 1:46-55

Over and over, the Gospel upends the assumptions of this world. Those who are rich and powerful receive their full reward here, but the poor and humble will receive a hundredfold in God's kingdom. While no generation has fully accepted this wisdom, none has rejected it as thoroughly as the modern world. Living in an age in which material riches abound, most find no need to be "poor in spirit"; being rich in the things of this world is considered the source of fulfillment and joy. The rich, the beautiful, and the powerful are exalted. How different everything must look in the eyes of God! Where modern society sees success and riches, he sees our poverty of soul. Those who are forgotten and ignored, but have come to a place in which all they desire is the Lord, are the most beautiful in the eyes of the Almighty. There is nothing to stand between them and the love of God. So much of modern society is consumed with the acquisition of material possessions, but the Lord's humble life should be a stark reminder that the things of this world do not equate to peace of heart or tranquility of soul.

In every age, God calls forth prophets — those who show the world a better path to holy living. Mother Teresa was that prophet in our times, specifically because she understood how to be evangelistically poor in spirit in an age of materialism and commercialism. By identifying with the material poor, she witnessed to the direct connection between the poor and Jesus. She liked to say of the poor, "Each one of them is Jesus in disguise." Modern man is enormously rich by any historical standard and has so much to prevent him from being like the Master, who had nowhere to lay his head (Mt 8:20). The goods of this world are not evil by nature (they are called "goods," after all), but they present a great temptation, distracting us from unadulterated service to Christ. Mother Teresa embraced a life of poverty, by her life proclaiming that all the things that are desired by the world — riches, possessions, beauty — are but dross in a life that is truly fulfilled.

Each attachment to this world weakens our attachment to Christ; the more numerous our material possessions, the more likely we are to form those attachments, and the more we will scrape and fight to maintain those attachments, even to the point of committing grave evil. The logic of materialism is brutally selfish. Personal comfort and happiness are put before anything — or anyone — who would get in the way. Mother Teresa had a clear view of one of the worst consequences of man's materialism:

> The greatest poverty in the world is killing a child so that you may live as you wish.

The rise of abortion in the modern world is directly tied to the materialism rampant in our culture. Moderns look upon the gift of a child — a blessing welcomed joyfully by those who are "poor in spirit" — as an intrusion in the accumulation of possessions. New life is a hindrance to a rich lifestyle. Instead of welcoming each child as a gift from God, many see these little ones as obstacles to a fulfilled life. Children are now a "disease" to be prevented by means of any drug or surgery necessary.

Materialism can afflict each of us in ways large and small. The perception of luxuries like a spacious house, two cars, and a college education as necessities may simply be rooted in a desire to be as materially blessed as our neighbors. These supposedly reasonable desires can, in fact, become obstacles to following Christ. The poverty of spirit Christ demands means a total detachment from the goods of this world, even those society assumes to be necessary.

How many people are called to live as missionaries, or in poorer areas of the country, but do not respond because of attachments to material things? How many youths is the Lord calling to religious life who will be unable to answer due to the crushing debts they acquired to live the "American dream"? Christ demands from each of his followers what he demanded of the rich young man: leave everything behind in order to follow him.

> "Truly, I say to you, it will be hard for a rich man to enter the kingdom of heaven. Again I tell you, it is easier for a camel to go through the eye of a needle than for a rich man to enter the kingdom of God."
>
> — Mt 19:23-24

True fulfillment and joy is becoming a "Nazarene" — a person who is poor in spirit, not attached to the things of this world; indeed, "set aside" from it. Those who would follow Jesus of Nazareth must imitate him by detaching themselves from the things that this world declares integral to a happy life. They will not receive a kingdom here, but Christ promises them much, much more:

> "Blessed are the poor in spirit, for theirs is the kingdom of heaven."
>
> — Mt 5:3

The reward that the poor in spirit receive makes the riches of this world look like so much refuse and waste. As she who is most poor in spirit proclaimed, God will surely "exalt those of low degree."

REFERENCES

Mt 2:23

For Reflection

- Am I inordinately attached to material things?
- Where in my life has the modern materialistic ethos blinded me to a disordered attachment to material things?

Shepherd

"I will strike the shepherd, and the sheep of the
flock will be scattered."

A country's national flag not only represents the nation; it also invokes in the country's inhabitants a great sense of patriotism, devotion, and unity. Just the sight of the flag can generate deep emotional feelings. Francis Scott Key was inspired to write *The Star-Spangled Banner* after seeing the flag still waving following a battle during the War of 1812, his relief and jubilation evident in the famous words, "Oh, say, does that star-spangled banner yet wave?" A simple piece of cloth transcends its nature to become an emotionally and historically charged symbol of unity among its people.

The Christian faith has far more than a symbol to unite it; it has the living person of Jesus Christ. Yet the unity that exists through Christ was sorely tested on the night before he died, when, as he predicted, his closest followers abandoned him. This, he said, would be the fulfillment of a prophecy found in the book of Zechariah:

> "You will all fall away because of me this night; for it is written, 'I will strike the shepherd, and the sheep of the flock will be scattered.'"

> — Mt 26:31, quoting Zech 13:7

Jesus is the apostles' source of unity; without his presence, they are simply lost sheep wandering without direction, as we can see by their reactions after his arrest in the Garden of Gethsemane. The apostles believed that under their own power they could follow Christ, even unto death. They learned with sorrow the insufficiency of their own strength.

Jesus, however, followed his prediction of their scattering with a promise that "after I am raised up, I will go before you to Galilee" (Mt 26:32). Jesus, like a good shepherd, does not abandon his followers for long, but remains with them always, even after his ascension to the Father. And his disciples will stay united if they "remain in" him.

In Acts, Luke relates that the Church in its earliest days was united in purpose and action:

> They devoted themselves to the apostles' teaching and fellowship, to the breaking of bread and the prayers.
>
> — Acts 2:42

This description shows the vital relationship between the "breaking of the bread" and achieving true fellowship. As the Shepherd of the Church, Jesus has remained with his sheep, keeping them united in one flock, primarily through the sacrament of the Eucharist — the "breaking of the bread," which is the sacrament of unity. The Eucharist binds the Church into a mystical communion that is impossible through any human means. Simply put, without the Eucharist, there is no Church: "The Eucharist makes the Church" (*CCC* 1395). Examining the history of the Church, one cannot but marvel that it still even exists today; the attacks from both within and without have been constant and, at times, brutal. From heresies arising from the bosom of the Church to persecutions launched by the state, the gates of hell have not relented in their assaults (cf. Mt 16:18). How could a purely human institution survive through the centuries against such opposition? But the Church has the benefit of a divine Shepherd who not only watches over his flock but gives his body as the very food by which it can remain united and strong.

From the very origins of the Church, her Eucharistic unity is clearly visible. St. Paul writes to the church in Corinth:

> The cup of blessing which we bless, is it not a participation in the blood of Christ? The bread which we break, is it not a participation in the body of Christ? Because there is one bread, we who are many are one body, for we all partake of the one bread.
>
> —1 Cor 10:16-18

It is through participation in the Eucharist that Christ's followers become more than just a likeminded group of people — they become one body. The Eucharist unites the Church to the saving act of Jesus on the cross, making her part of the world's redemption.

The Eucharist binds its recipients not only to the Lord but also to each other. In a very real way, the bond a partaker of the Eucharist has with his fellow communicants is deeper than that of flesh and blood. Biological unity is of the flesh, but Eucharistic unity is of the Spirit of God. Christ said in his Eucharistic discourse, "It is the spirit that gives life, the flesh is of no avail" (Jn 6:63). Each member of the Church is a true brother and sister in the Lord, and the Church is the family of God. A family may have arguments or disagreements, but nothing can make two of its members cease to be part of the same family. Likewise, the Church cannot be divided as long as it is united in the Eucharist.

This unity is not uniformity, as there is a wonderful diversity always present in the Church. Like a body, the Church has members who are hands and feet and all parts of the body, but all must — through the Eucharist — operate as one body. However, once men believe the Church can remain one flock without the Shepherd — i.e., without the Eucharist — they are doomed to relive the tower of

Babel, an arrogant pursuit that led to disorder and disunity.

Unity is something everyone desires; who wants to be part of disorder, after all? Yet the means to achieve unity is frequently misunderstood. Often, Christians picture unity as simple doctrinal agreement: if we all accept the same theology, then we are united, correct? However, unity in the Church is not the result of theological conformity; rather, theological agreement is the result of a preexisting unity founded upon the Eucharist. It is not coincidental that the greatest case of disunity in the Church — the sixteenth-century Protestant Reformation — included a denigration of the Eucharist to merely a symbol of Christ rather than his real Presence. No longer bound by the Eucharist, the leaders of the Reformation began a never-ending proliferation of new denominations and Christian bodies.

The Church is not united based on the desires and strengths of men, but because of the unifying grace of the Eucharist. Without it, our fallen race is guaranteed to be divided. Thus, those who are still united through the Eucharist should not look upon these sad events in a spirit of pride or triumphalism; it is not of man's power that the Church remains united. Only — *only* — by the presence of the Shepherd in the Eucharist can it hope to remain one flock. Without him as the source of unity, his followers will truly be a flock that is scattered.

Reception of the Eucharist, however, is not a magic potion that ensures unity. Judas was present at the Last Supper and received the Lord in the Eucharist, yet he still betrayed Christ. We must receive the Eucharist in a spirit of humility, with a heart open to being led by God. St. Paul warns:

> Whoever, therefore, eats the bread or drinks the cup of the Lord in an unworthy manner will be guilty of profaning the body and blood of the Lord. Let a man examine himself, and so eat of the bread and drink of the cup. For any one who

eats and drinks without discerning the body eats and drinks
judgment upon himself.

— 1 Cor 11:27-29

Receiving the Eucharist without a spirit of docility leads to
condemnation, not unity. Having a shepherd, by definition, means
that we are sheep. But a sheep that believes he can lead the flock
brings only disaster to himself and his brethren. We must receive
the Eucharist with the recognition of ourselves as sheep who are
lost without Christ, our Shepherd.

One of the primary ways to exercise this humility is in the
attitude we have toward the shepherds Christ has given on earth
to lead his sheep in his stead. We saw earlier that the united
Church devoted itself to the "apostles' teachings" (Acts 4:42): it was
accepted by all that the apostles were charged with the ministry of
teaching the Gospel. Matthew tells us that the apostolic ministry
given to him and his fellow apostles comes from Jesus himself:

> "All authority in heaven and on earth has been given to me. Go
> therefore and make disciples of all nations, baptizing them in
> the name of the Father and of the Son and of the Holy Spirit,
> *teaching them to observe all that I have commanded you*; and lo, I
> am with you always, to the close of the age."
>
> — Mt 28:18-20 (emphasis added)

Followers of Christ are obligated to "observe" — to obey — the
shepherds Christ has placed over them and abide by their teachings.
The apostles, and their successors, the bishops, have been given
Christ's authority to preach, to teach, and to guide his flock here
on earth. His flock cannot simply ignore these shepherds and go its
own way. To do so is to ignore the Good Shepherd himself.

One of the mysteries here is the deep connection between the
Eucharist and obedience to the bishops as shepherds. Without
communion through the Eucharist, submission to the bishops
is not possible, because that submission requires grace. Without

obedience to the bishops, reception of the Eucharist becomes an individual act divorced from its meaning, an "unworthy" reception that brings judgment on the recipient (cf. 1 Cor 11:27-29).

The early second-century bishop and disciple of John the apostle, St. Ignatius of Antioch, witnessed the passing of the apostles to their heavenly reward. But he knew that the Lord would not leave his Church without shepherds to guide them. The bishops, he taught, were to be the new shepherds, succeeding the apostles in this ministry. Surely there were those who desired to go their own way after the apostles died. But Ignatius, who had learned the Faith at the feet of the Lord's beloved disciple, knew that union with the bishops was a necessary component of following Christ. Furthermore, the Eucharist — the source of true unity — was entrusted only to the bishops as the successors to the apostles. On his way to martyrdom, Ignatius wrote to the church in Smyrna:

> But avoid all divisions, as the beginning of evils. See that you all follow the bishop, even as Jesus Christ does the Father, and the presbytery as you would the apostles; and reverence the deacons, as being the institution of God. Let no man do anything connected with the Church without the bishop. Let that be deemed a proper Eucharist, which is [administered] either by the bishop, or by one to whom he has entrusted it. Wherever the bishop shall appear, there let the multitude [of the people] also be; even as, wherever Jesus Christ is, there is the Catholic Church. It is not lawful without the bishop either to baptize or to celebrate a love-feast; but whatsoever he shall approve of, that is also pleasing to God, so that everything that is done may be secure and valid.
>
> — *Letter to the Smyrnaeans* 7-8[21]

The people must be united to the bishop, as this is how the Church is united to Christ. Christ, in his love, has given his flock shepherds here on earth to keep us united to him. To maintain that unity, his followers must be devoted to the bishops' teachings, as the first Christians were.

Furthermore, Jesus has given himself in the Eucharist as our food to give us the strength we need to follow these shepherds. If a shepherd were to take his sheep on a long journey, he would ensure that they would have plenty of food along the way. Christ, the Good Shepherd, gives his sheep his very life as food. This food gives us strength to follow our shepherd no matter where he leads — through trial and tribulation, sorrow and mourning. On the night he gave the Church the Eucharist, Jesus predicted that the flock would be scattered, fulfilling Zechariah's prophecy. But by his very actions that night, the rest of the prophecy would also come true:

> And I will . . . refine them as one refines silver, and test them as gold is tested. They will call on my name, and I will answer them. I will say, "They are my people"; and they will say, "The LORD is my God."

— Zech 13:9

REFERENCES

Mt 26:31

For Reflection

- Is the Eucharist the center of my spiritual life? Through it, do I allow myself to be conformed to the teachings of the Church?

- How can I increase my reverence for our Lord in the Eucharist?

Physician

"Those who are well have no need of a physician,
but those who are sick."

Stories of personal conversion comprise one of the most powerful genres of religious literature. St. Augustine's *Confessions,* a classic example of this type of work, has become the most influential text of its kind in the Western world. Its beauty and depth are evident in its opening words:

> You are great, Lord, and highly to be praised: great is your power and your wisdom is immeasurable. Man, a little piece of your creation, desires to praise you, a human being bearing his mortality with him, carrying with him the witness of his sin and the witness that you resist the proud. Nevertheless, to praise you is the desire of man, a little piece of your creation. You stir man to take pleasure in praising you, because you have made us for yourself, and our heart is restless until it rests in you.[22]

More people have probably been drawn to the Christian Faith by St. Augustine's book than any other story of personal conversion. More recently, John Henry Newman's *Apologia Pro Vita Sua* has convinced many English-speaking intellectuals of the truth and beauty of the Catholic faith. Of course, St. Paul's conversion is considered foundational to the origins of the Church; Luke finds it so important that he relates it on three separate occasions in Acts. And Matthew's story of his own conversion is perhaps the most personal account found in the four Gospels (Mt 9:9-13). In typical Gospel fashion, the narrative is short and modest, yet it reveals a profound self-understanding and a deep dependence upon Jesus.

The story really begins when the Evangelist, after recounting the core of Jesus' preaching in the Sermon on the Mount, begins to detail the other pillar of Jesus' public ministry: healing the sick, the lame, and the possessed. Beginning in Chapter 8 and culminating in the story of the paralytic in 9:1-8, Matthew describes the healing of a leper, the cure of a centurion's servant, the restoration of Peter's mother-in-law, and the exorcism of two demoniacs. The disease of the person or method used by Jesus does not matter — the result is the same: instant healing.

But it is the curing of the paralytic that reveals the heart of Jesus' healing ministry:

> And getting into a boat he crossed over and came to his own city. And behold, they brought to him a paralytic, lying on his bed; and when Jesus saw their faith he said to the paralytic, "Take heart, my son; your sins are forgiven." And behold, some of the scribes said to themselves, "This man is blaspheming." But Jesus, knowing their thoughts, said, "Why do you think evil in your hearts? For which is easier, to say, 'Your sins are forgiven,' or to say, 'Rise and walk'? But that you may know that the Son of man has authority on earth to forgive sins" — he then said to the paralytic — "Rise, take up your bed and go home." And he rose and went home. When the crowds saw it, they were afraid, and they glorified God, who had given such authority to men.
>
> — Mt 9:1-8

The priority for Jesus as healer is the healing of the soul from the one disease that can afflict it: sin. The paralytic came looking for physical healing, but like any physician, Jesus looked beyond his patient's surface problems to focus on the real crisis. By doing so, he could bring complete and total healing for the man, body and soul.

Sin is the most paralyzing force there is. It obstructs our

freedom to be children of God. Paul speaks of the "slavery to sin" and the need to be freed through Christ to be a son or daughter of God. Forgiveness is the only medicine that can cure this paralysis; without it, guilt and shame weigh down the conscience, holding it prisoner to regrets and recriminations. Jesus understands this reality. By granting forgiveness to the paralytic, he heals him in a much deeper way than simple physical healing could.

The paralytic himself may not have understood his need. A person going to a doctor may only be aware of symptoms without understanding the underlying cause. A good physician, however, studies the symptoms in order to diagnose and treat the real disease. It would be foolish for the patient to argue with the doctor for not treating the symptoms directly. Likewise, when going to the Lord for healing, it is foolish to reject the medicine he prescribes. It might mean that the suffering present isn't alleviated, but perhaps that suffering is a path to greater intimacy with Christ, and the Lord doesn't want it to be removed for that reason. It might be through that suffering that the greatest healing can occur. It is the physician's decision as to the course of treatment, not the patient's.

Immediately after the story of the paralytic, Matthew recounts his own calling. This context is important: he has established Jesus as a true healer of body and soul to lay the groundwork for his own transformation.

> As Jesus passed on from there, he saw a man called Matthew sitting at the tax office; and he said to him, "Follow me." And he rose and followed him.
>
> And as he sat at table in the house, behold, many tax collectors and sinners came and sat down with Jesus and his disciples. And when the Pharisees saw this, they said to his disciples, "Why does your teacher eat with tax collectors and sinners?" But when he heard it, he said, "Those who are well have no need of a physician, but those who are sick. Go and learn what

> this means, 'I desire mercy, and not sacrifice.' For I came not to
> call the righteous, but sinners."
>
> — Mt 9:9-13

Here, Matthew is defending his apostolic call against those who might question a tax collector as one of Christ's closest collaborators. As a tax collector, Matthew has the most despised of jobs: he not only had to interact with "unclean" peoples, but he also worked for the hated Romans. And if Matthew was like most tax collectors of his time, he collected taxes above the Roman rate in order to line his own pockets. On the Jewish social scale, he was no better than a prostitute — yet Jesus personally called him to be one of his inner circle of followers.

The beauty of this conversion story lies in Matthew's recognition of his own state — he knows he is a "sinner," yet he rejoices that his sinfulness has brought forth the great mercy of Christ. Furthermore, he is telling his readers that all who would follow Christ must first recognize their own sinfulness. Christ is not interested in the "righteous" — he wants to call sinners to his table and bring them to salvation.

One of our most common ailments may very well be that we do not see ourselves as one of the sinners, but as the righteous. This is no less true of those in the Church. By outwardly following the precepts of the Church, we may consider ourselves above those who explicitly reject the Church's teachings, such as those who engage in homosexuality or other sexual immorality. Yet we are no less sinners than they, in need of Christ's redemption. If a person does not think he is spiritually sick, why go to the Physician of souls? Matthew is trying to remind his readers who they are in the eyes of God: sinners in need of redemption. But God looks at "sinners" in mercy, not judgment; the mercy of a father who was willing to give up his only Son in order to restore his children to health.

The early Church Fathers, especially in the East, were particularly devoted to the image of Jesus as the Divine Physician. Clement of Alexandria writes:

> The good Instructor, the Wisdom, the Word of the Father, who made man, cares for the whole nature of His creature; the all-sufficient Physician of humanity, the Saviour, heals both body and soul. "Rise up," He said to the paralytic; "take the bed on which you lie, and go away home;" and straightway the infirm man received strength. And to the dead He said, "Lazarus, go forth;" and the dead man issued from his coffin such as he was ere he died, having undergone resurrection. Further, He heals the soul itself by precepts and gifts - by precepts indeed, in course of time, but being liberal in His gifts, He says to us sinners, "Your sins be forgiven you."
>
> — *The Instructor, Book 1*, Chapter 2[23]

Clement recognizes the unity of the body and soul within each person.

The Church has always had to battle against forces within her that attempt to denigrate the body, or to establish a didactic of body/soul dualism. Christianity, however, is an Incarnational faith. Christ in his Incarnation united his divine Person to a body, and in so doing, redeemed the physical world. Historically, when groups like the Gnostics have tried to disconnect the human person from the body — believing that the body is either unnecessary or inherently evil — two extremes developed: on one side, a total asceticism, and on the other, a libertine attitude. For if the body has no relationship to the soul, what one does with the body becomes isolated from a person's spiritual development. Yet the Church teaches that man is fundamentally a unity of body and soul, and Jesus, as the Divine Physician, looks to cure both. His healing ministry did not just consist of spiritual healings, although they had priority; he also healed bodily ailments. These two aspects of man, body and soul, must remain in communion in order for man to be truly human.

The actions of the saints throughout the ages witness to this dynamic. Physical healings abound in their biographies, and these healings do not merely point to God's power in their lives: they are true acts of mercy in which people are freed by the saint's actions from an affliction that weighs them down. Christ's physical healings are instances of the mercy of God piercing the world, touching the body to draw the soul closer to him.

Only when we are in harmony with God do we experience true harmony between body and soul. We were created as a body-soul composite, intended to be in union with our Creator, and the union between God and man effects a union within our own being. Thus, sin is the ultimate attack against the natural unity between body and soul, and each sin committed causes great harm to both.

But the Divine Physician, in his great mercy, has given us a remedy to this disease in the sacraments. These seven gifts are the highest reflection of the body/spirit unity that exists in the life of Christ, God made man. Like the Incarnation, each sacrament is a physical reality that God's presence makes spiritually beneficial. The Fathers saw the sacraments, especially the Eucharist, as the medicine Christ uses to cure the deepest ailments of man. St. Ignatius of Antioch called the Eucharist "the medicine of immortality, and the antidote to prevent us from dying, but [which causes] that we should live for ever in Jesus Christ" (*Letter to the Ephesians* 10). The Eucharist is the divine food that strengthens us against sin and temptation:

> As bodily nourishment restores lost strength, so the Eucharist strengthens our charity, which tends to be weakened in daily life.
>
> — *CCC* 1394

The other sacraments also heal the disunity caused by sin. Baptism removes all sin and gives new life to its recipient. Confession repairs the harm sin causes and restores the soul to health. And through the sacrament of the Anointing of the Sick, the Divine Physician gives his patients the grace to accept their injuries and afflictions. Although Jesus no longer walks the earth as he did in first-century Palestine, he has left his Church with his healing medicine to cure and heal each person of the infirmities that afflict him.

We all seek healing for our afflictions, spiritual and physical, and Matthew's encounter with Christ is a model for meeting the Divine Physician. Recognizing the need for healing, the Christian places himself in the hands of the merciful Lord. The prayer of the ancient *Divine Liturgy of the Holy Apostle and Evangelist Mark* beautifully reflects the disposition each Christian should have toward Christ:

> But do Thou, O Lord, the physician of our souls and bodies, the guardian of all flesh, look down, and by Thy saving power heal all the diseases of soul and body.

REFERENCES
Mt 9:12

For Reflection
- Where do I need healing?
- Do I take this need to Jesus, the Divine Physician, and trust that he can heal me?

Bridegroom

"Can the wedding guests mourn as long as the bridegroom is with them?"

To a groom on his wedding day, the sight of his bride walking down the aisle is the most beautiful of images. This is the person to whom he is giving his life, the person to whom he will be united until the end of his life. His future wife is lovely beyond all telling.

> Behold, you are beautiful, my love, behold, you are beautiful! Your eyes are doves behind your veil. . . . You are all fair, my love; there is no flaw in you.
>
> — Song 4:1, 7

The sacramental union of a man and woman is the most intimate earthly union possible. As Genesis says:

> Therefore a man leaves his father and his mother and cleaves to his wife, and they become one flesh.
>
> — Gen 2:24

No longer are the two separate, but now they are one in desire, purpose, and body.

Recognizing the depth of the marital union helps us understand more fully one of the primary images for God in the Old Testament: a bridegroom whose bride is the nation of Israel. The prophet Isaiah describes the Lord like this:

> For your Maker is your husband,
>   the Lord of hosts is his name;

and the Holy One of Israel is your Redeemer,
    the God of the whole earth he is called.

— Is 54:5

And, he exclaims:

For as a young man marries a virgin,
    so shall your sons marry you,
and as the bridegroom rejoices over the bride,
    so shall your God rejoice over you.

— Is 62:5

The prophet Hosea also compares the Lord to a husband who longs for his wife:

And in that day, says the LORD, you will call me, "My husband" . . . And I will betroth you to me for ever; I will betroth you to me in righteousness and in justice, in steadfast love, and in mercy. I will betroth you to me in faithfulness; and you shall know the LORD.

— Hos 2:16, 19-20

This imagery is all the more powerful coming from Hosea. He was married to a woman who was not only unfaithful to their marriage promises; she was a temple prostitute. The prophet's marriage to this unfaithful spouse was a flesh-and-blood analogy of the Lord's marriage to Israel. The Lord told Hosea:

"Go again, love a woman who is beloved of a paramour and is an adulteress; even as the LORD loves the people of Israel, though they turn to other gods and love cakes of raisins."

— Hos 3:1

Imagine the pain and hurt the prophet must have felt over his wife's actions, which reflected the unfaithfulness of Israel toward the Lord. Though his wife did not deserve it, Hosea stayed with her, signifying how the Lord would always remain with Israel despite her adulterous idolatry.

During the Roman occupation, this image of God as the faithful bridegroom of Israel was especially consoling to the Jewish people. They knew that, throughout their hardships and trials, God was a faithful spouse who would never abandon his bride, Israel. The title "bridegroom" became a revered symbol of God's steadfastness toward his chosen people. Because of this historic sacred imagery, the Jews are astounded to hear Jesus' response to the challenge from John the Baptist's disciples about his disciples' lack of fasting:

> "Can the wedding guests mourn as long as the bridegroom is with them? The days will come, when the bridegroom is taken away from them, and then they will fast."
>
> — Mt 9:15

Jesus has placed himself in the role of bridegroom, thus appropriating one of the most cherished titles given to God. Following closely after he had claimed to forgive a man's sins (Mt 9:2), this self-identification further intensifies the tension between him and the Jewish leaders. Jesus was making incredible — and possibly blasphemous — claims about himself.

The link Jesus proposes between the bridegroom and fasting is not an arbitrary one, either. In using this imagery in regard to the discipline of fasting, Jesus reminds his listeners of the dual purpose of this penitential practice: to recognize the sad reality of our separation from our divine bridegroom, and to draw closer to him through denial of one's passions. The apostles had no need to fast while in the presence of Jesus, since his presence brought them into a joyful communion with the Father.

Yet Christians after the Ascension are called to fast; Jesus says there will be a time to fast "when the bridegroom is taken away from them," and in his Sermon on the Mount, he presupposes that his followers will fast (Mt 6:16-18). And fast they did. In the first-century manual on Christian living called the *Didache*, Christians are advised to fast on Wednesdays and Fridays (*Didache* 8:1). Jesus specifically tells his disciples that fasting, along with prayer, is required to drive out certain unclean spirits (Mt 17:21). Fasting is an obligation of all followers of Christ.

Denying oneself physical sustenance is an acknowledgement of the Fall, for it was through the Fall that man was separated from God and his bodily needs took inordinate control of him. Thus, fasting presupposes mourning. It recognizes that God's intention is for man to be like pre-lapsian Adam and Eve: in control of his body and united to God. Because the apostles were in the presence of Christ, they were filled with joy by the union it brought them with God and had no need to fast to draw closer to him. But in this passage, Jesus gives his first hint that the road to redemption will lead through the Passion: the bridegroom — Jesus — will not always be with them, but will have to allow others to take him away in order that salvation might come.

The image of Christ as bridegroom became a primary one for the primitive Church. St. Paul declares in his letter to the Ephesians:

> For the husband is the head of the wife as Christ is the head of the church, his body, and is himself its Savior. . . . Husbands, love your wives, as Christ loved the church and gave himself up for her, that he might sanctify her, having cleansed her by the washing of water with the word, that he might present the church to himself in splendor, without spot or wrinkle or any such thing, that she might be holy and without blemish. . . . For no man ever hates his own flesh, but nourishes and cherishes it, as Christ does the church, because we are members of his body. "For this reason a man shall leave his father and mother and be joined to his wife, and the two shall become one flesh." This mystery is a profound one, and I am saying that it refers to Christ and the church.
>
> — Eph 5:23, 25-27, 29-32

The Church is now the bride of Christ, and Christ loves his bride as his own body. Just as a husband should consider his wife as part of his own body, so the Church, the bride of Christ, is also Christ's body. And it is Christ's love which makes the Church "holy": "Husbands, love your wives, as Christ loved the church and gave himself up for her, that he might sanctify her . . . that she might be holy and without blemish," St. Paul writes.

One of the traditional marks of the Church is that she is holy. However, a common misinterpretation of this text from Paul is that all the Church's *members* are holy — but simple experience (and self-examination) reveal that this is not the case. Thus many people, including many Christians, simply deny the holiness of the Church . . . although the creed tells us otherwise. The holiness of the Church comes from Christ's self-sacrifice for her. As a husband sees his wife as spotless on their wedding day, so Christ sees the Church. This is no illusion; Christ's very *desire* that she be holy *makes* her holy, as his sacrificial blood washes her clean.

John's vision in the book of Revelation of the consummation of all things shows that the reality of the Church as bride and Christ as bridegroom will endure for all eternity.

> And I saw the holy city, new Jerusalem, coming down out of heaven from God, prepared as a bride adorned for her husband. . . . Then came one of the seven angels who had the seven bowls full of the seven last plagues, and spoke to me, saying, "Come, I will show you the Bride, the wife of the Lamb."
>
> — Rev 21:2, 9

The Church will enjoy a perpetual honeymoon with the Lord, deeply united with him for all time. The "one flesh" of marital union is thus a mere shadow of the union that we will enjoy in heaven with God and with all the saints. The beatific vision will allow us to see God "face-to-face"; no longer will he be hidden under the appearance of bread or represented by the priest. He will be all in all, and as his bride, we will be intimately united to him.

One must be prepared for this day, for Christ's parable of the wedding feast shows that only those who are invited and prepared will enjoy it:

> And again Jesus spoke to them in parables, saying, "The kingdom of heaven may be compared to a king who gave a marriage feast for his son, and sent his servants to call those who were invited to the marriage feast; but they would not come. Again he sent other servants, saying, 'Tell those who are invited, Behold, I have made ready my dinner, my oxen and my fat calves are killed, and everything is ready; come to the marriage feast.' But they made light of it and went off, one to his farm, another to his business, while the rest seized his servants, treated them shamefully, and killed them. The king was angry, and he sent his troops and destroyed those murderers and burned their city. Then he said to his servants, 'The wedding is ready, but those invited were not worthy. Go therefore to the thoroughfares, and invite to the marriage feast as many as you find.' And those servants went out into the streets and gathered all whom they found, both bad and good; so the wedding hall was filled with guests.
>
> "But when the king came in to look at the guests, he saw there a man who had no wedding garment; and he said to him, 'Friend, how did you get in here without a wedding garment?' And he was speechless. Then the king said to the attendants, 'Bind him hand and foot, and cast him into the outer darkness; there men will weep and gnash their teeth.'
>
> "For many are called, but few are chosen."
>
> — Mt 22:1-14

Why does the king throw out the man who is not properly attired? Wedding etiquette of that time required that a guest wear clean white clothes — clothes that were available to anyone. So when this man was invited off the street, he should have returned home first to change before arriving at the wedding. Instead, he presumed upon his host's generosity and arrived in his work clothes.

Likewise, although everyone is offered a free invitation to

the wedding feast of the Lamb, the guests still have "clothing" obligations to fulfill. In the Christian life, the invitation is the gift of faith (freely given by God) and the clean white clothing is the life of charity (chosen by us). St. Gregory the Great wrote:

> What then must we understand by the wedding garment but love? . . . He may have faith, but does not have love. We are correct when we say that love is the wedding garment because this is what our Creator himself possessed when he came to the marriage feast to join the church to himself. Only God's love brought it about that his only begotten Son united the hearts of his chosen to himself.
>
> — *Forty Gospel Homilies* 38.9[24]

Faith is the invitation that brings us to the feast; to be part of the wedding, we must act out that faith in works of charity. As James declares:

> What does it profit, my brethren, if a man says he has faith but has not works? Can his faith save him? If a brother or sister is ill-clad and in lack of daily food, and one of you says to them, "Go in peace, be warmed and filled," without giving them the things needed for the body, what does it profit? So faith by itself, if it has no works, is dead.
>
> — Jas 2:14-17

In order to be properly attired and accepted as a wedding guest, the Christian must live a life of "faith working through love" (Gal 5:5). In the parable, the guest does nothing to be invited, but is sent away if he does not follow the desires of the host. And the host is God, who is love (1 Jn 4:8). Our Lord warned in Matthew 7:21:

> "Not every one who says to me, 'Lord, Lord,' shall enter the kingdom of heaven, but he who does the will of my Father who is in heaven."

The will of the one who is Love is love: to serve the poor and needy, to show the lost the path to salvation, and to sacrifice one's own good for the good of others. This is how one garbs himself for the wedding feast of the Lamb, in the clean white clothes of love. This proper attire is reflected in the traditional garment of the newly-baptized: a white robe that represents the pure love of God which infuses the soul at baptism, allowing the new Christian to respond in love toward God and others.

Christ is the bridegroom who passionately loves his bride. He gave his very life to save her. In response, those who are invited to the wedding feast must love Christ in return, willingly giving their lives to him. What bride would not do so for her beloved?

REFERENCES

Mt 9:15

For Reflection

- How seriously do I take Christ's call to holiness?
- Am I satisfied with just "getting by," or do I strive to model my life after Christ?
- Do I do this with the joy of a bride and bridegroom?

Emmanuel

"His name shall be called Emmanuel (which means,
God with us)."

During Advent, the writings of the prophet Isaiah take center stage, dominating the Old Testament readings chosen for both the Mass and the Office of Readings. These readings remind their hearers of the deep longing of the people of the Old Covenant for a redeemer, one who would re-establish their intimate relationship with God. Within these writings, a single name bursts through the shadows of the Old Testament to enlighten and define the whole season: Emmanuel.

Isaiah declares that one day will come the son of a virgin whose very name will be "God with us" (cf. Is 7:14). Intimacy with God, ruptured since Adam's Fall, will be restored. The Christmas mystery revolves around this promise, and Matthew is thus quick to apply it to the babe to be born in Bethlehem:

> "Joseph, son of David, do not fear to take Mary your wife, for that which is conceived in her is of the Holy Spirit; she will bear a son, and you shall call his name Jesus, for he will save his people from their sins." All this took place to fulfil what the Lord had spoken by the prophet: "Behold, a virgin shall conceive and bear a son, and his name shall be called Emmanuel" (which means, God with us).
>
> — Mt 1:20-23

The centuries-old longing of the Jewish people will be fulfilled beyond all their dreams and desires. God will not simply raise up another great prophet in the tradition of Elijah or Jeremiah. He will not grant mere political success to a strong leader like David or Judas Maccabeus. No, God will now send his only Son to be with his people. Intimacy with God will reach depths as yet unknown — God will truly be with humanity, suffering with them, rejoicing with them, and living day-in and day-out with them. Even the herald of the original prophecy, Isaiah, would never have dreamed of such a gift from the Almighty. Under the Old Covenant, only one man, once a year, was allowed to enter the Holy of Holies and thus be given direct access to God. With the coming of Emmanuel, a truly new era was to begin: now, every man and woman, slave and free, Jew and Gentile, would be given direct access to God through Jesus Christ.

But a careful reader notices a discrepancy in the passage quoted from Matthew above: immediately after the angel pronounces that the child's name is to be Jesus, which means "God saves," Matthew writes that this fulfills the prophecy of Isaiah that he will be called "Emmanuel," which means "God with us." So what is his name to be — Jesus, or Emmanuel? Has he come to be an instrument of God's salvation or to bring God to us? The answer is both, for the two names have two separate purposes: the first indicates *what* God will do through his Son, and the second is *how* God will do it. It is through the Incarnation that Salvation is brought to man.

In the Garden of Eden, humanity enjoyed complete familiarity with God, a closeness that was destroyed when man attempted to be "like God" (Gen 3:5). But in a most wondrous irony, God's plan of salvation now brings about the very thing that man sinfully desired: the elevation of humanity to his divine likeness. God is not simply restoring humanity to Adam's original blessed state; he is allowing it, through union with him, to be transformed into his likeness. Like iron in a furnace that begins to take upon itself the characteristics of the fire, man's union with God transforms man into the divine image. All this becomes possible through the Incarnation.

In the Easter *Exultet*, the Church rejoices that our "happy fault," our "necessary sin," was transformed by "so great a Redeemer" — that God's infinite goodness, the salvation he brings about in consequence of Adam's Fall, raises the human race to heights unimagined. God lowers himself to man's level, but only in order to raise man up. As St. Athanasius famously stated, "The Son of God became man so that men might be become sons of God."

Emmanuel means "God with us," but his task is to make humanity eventually be with God — and by being with God, become like God. The mystery of the Incarnation, summed up in the name *Emmanuel*, is that by taking on a human nature, God elevates human nature, by grace, to "partake of the divine nature" (2 Pet 1:4). In the Christian East, this process of transformation is called "*theosis*," or "deification." God's irresponsible love pours forth in this mystery: the human race, which has endlessly rebelled against God and petulantly rejected him time and again, is given the greatest possible (or even impossible) gift and is raised to perfection through Christ.

Matthew's linking together the names "Emmanuel" and "Jesus" thus introduces the reader to the very *raison d'être* of the Christian message: that God's condescension to humanity occurred to bring about humanity's ascension to union with, and participation in, his divinity. This fundamental truth is proclaimed by saints and fathers both West and East. St. Thomas Aquinas grasps, in the divine plan to raise men up, the inherent humility of God:

> To restore man, who has been laid low by sin, to the heights of divine glory, the Word of the eternal Father, though containing all things within His immensity, willed to become small…The humanity of Christ is the way by which we come to the divinity.
> — *Compendium of Theology*[25]

Likewise, St. Maximus the Confessor appreciates the means by which man's final destination will be achieved:

> A sure warrant for looking forward with hope to deification of
> human nature is provided by the Incarnation of God, which
> makes man god to the same degree as God himself became man.
>
> — *Philokalia* Vol. II[26]

The Christian faith for 2,000 years has rejoiced that the emptying of God in the Incarnation results in the final exaltation of man into his image.

St. Paul understood that the transformation that is the destiny of all Christians is beyond our ability to comprehend:

> No eye has seen, no ear has heard, no mind has conceived what
> God has prepared for those who love him.
>
> — 1 Cor 2:9

The apostle eagerly anticipates the transformation awaiting the followers of Christ, seeing in this work the metamorphosis of all of creation from decay to life:

> [C]reation waits with eager longing for the revealing of the
> sons of God . . . the creation itself will be set free from its
> bondage to decay and obtain the glorious liberty of the children
> of God. We know that the whole creation has been groaning
> in travail together until now; and not only the creation, but we
> ourselves, who have the first fruits of the Spirit, groan inwardly
> as we wait for adoption as sons, the redemption of our bodies.
>
> — Rom 8:18-23

Creation "waits with eager longing"; it is "groaning in travail"; we "groan inwardly"; Paul is beside himself in anticipation of what lies ahead for God's people. He knows that man is incapable of grasping the totality of his destiny:

> For now we see in a mirror dimly, but then face to face. Now I
> know in part; then I shall understand fully, even as I have been
> fully understood.
>
> — 1 Cor 13:12

Human words — even from a Shakespeare, or a Keats, or even the inspired Word of God — cannot adequately describe our final end. Yet this is the fate that man has been created for, the fate for which he is intended to live.

But the transformation that is in store for the followers of Christ does not begin after this life is over. The metamorphosis into the likeness of divinity — by means of union — begins here on earth, at baptism. Baptism is the initiation of this transformation, when man's participation in divine life begins. St. Paul writes:

> Do you not know that all of us who have been baptized into Christ Jesus were baptized into his death? . . . For if we have been united with him in a death like his, we shall certainly be united with him in a resurrection like his. . . . if we have died with Christ, we believe that we shall also live with him.
>
> — Rom 6:3, 5, 8

The Christian is not baptized "for Christ" or "like Christ"; he is baptized "into Christ." By the immersion into the water, the believer enters into the very life of God, receiving the grace necessary to transform his human nature into the likeness of divinity. It was through his obedient suffering and death that Christ was glorified by the Father (cf. Jn 17); therefore, his followers participate in this glory by uniting themselves to his death via baptism, and thus also receive the fruits of his obedience in his resurrection. Baptism thus becomes the first step in *theosis*.

The union with Christ that begins at baptism is deepened and strengthened by participation in the Eucharist. St Paul asks:

> The cup of blessing which we bless, is it not a participation (*koinonia*) in the blood of Christ? The bread which we break, is it not a participation (*koinonia*) in the body of Christ?
>
> — 1 Cor 10:16

The term Paul uses here — *koinonia* — connotes a deep intimacy and union. The communicant is not simply reflecting or even contemplating Christ when he receives the Eucharist; he becomes more intimate with Christ than even a man and his wife can be with one another. Yet Paul also includes a warning in this passage: through the Eucharist, one becomes united to the "blood of Christ." This tells us that suffering and self-denial are necessary components to union with Christ — that one cannot be intimate with Christ without being intimate with his Passion. As Christ had to suffer and die in order to enter into his glory, so also must his followers. The path to Easter Sunday must always go through Good Friday first. The deeper our union with Christ on the cross, the deeper will be our union with Christ in his glory.

The Eucharist, by bringing about this *koinonia*, is truly the "Emmanuel sacrament": Jesus is with his people in an inimitable and mysterious way. In yet another example of God's reckless love, he gives his Son away each time the faithful receive the Eucharist. The communicant becomes sacramentally united with the Lord of Lords, through whom the universe was made. As the prophecy of Isaiah became reality in the womb of the Virgin Mary, so it is realized again in each act of Holy Communion.

The union effected by reception of the Eucharist continues the process of transformation into the divine image. St. Augustine expresses the intention of Christ:

> "I am the food of the fully grown; grow and you will feed on me. And you will not change me into you like the food your flesh eats, but you will be changed into me."
>
> — *Confessions* 7:10[27]

The small host of the Eucharist, as we consume it physically, consumes us spiritually, transforming us into the likeness of that which is being eaten: Jesus Christ.

This is what Jesus means when he proclaims:

> "Truly, truly, I say to you, unless you eat the flesh of the Son of man and drink his blood, you have no life in you; he who eats

my flesh and drinks my blood has eternal life, and I will raise
him up at the last day."

— Jn 6:53-54

What is "eternal life"? Jesus tells us later, in John 17:3:

"And this is eternal life, that they know thee the only true God,
and Jesus Christ whom thou hast sent."

But what does it mean to "know" God? Biblically, the concept
of knowing is much more than intellectual knowledge; it is deep
intimate union. As such, "knowing" is often used to refer to sexual
intimacy. The Eucharist mystically effects this deep knowledge of
God within the lives of the communicants, thus allowing us to have
a share in eternal life. Each reception of the Eucharist becomes a
reliving of the Christmas mystery; and as Christ's presence in this
world as "God with us" transformed all of history, so, too, does his
presence transform the receiver of this great gift.

REFERENCES

Mt 1:23

For Reflection

- Do my words and actions reflect the great dignity I have as
  an image of God?
- In what areas of my life might I need to make changes in
  order to more fully "partake of the divine nature"?

Son of Abraham

The book of . . . Jesus Christ . . . the son of
Abraham.

Modern society's unique attributes are many, but one of its saddest must be its deprecation of previous generations: never before has a culture so rejected those who came before it. Ancient cultures — and even those just previous to ours — valued their roots and had great respect for their forefathers. These generations emphasized the importance of a family's heritage. The patriarch's word was law within a family, and family members of previous generations were venerated.

So it was in ancient Jewish culture. The opening chapters of Genesis contain many genealogies in order to emphasize the roots of the great Jewish patriarchs. The first eight chapters of 1 Chronicles are made up almost entirely of the genealogies of the twelve tribes of Israel, reminding readers where they came from.

This veneration of ancestors was also present in Roman society; one of the difficulties for the first preachers of the Christian Gospel was the contempt many Romans felt for "new" religions. Only those religions that could date back many centuries were considered legitimate; new faiths were suspect. The first great apologist of the Church, St. Justin Martyr, wrote in such an atmosphere:

> Reason directs those who are truly pious and philosophical to honor and love only what is true, declining to follow traditional opinions, if these be worthless. For not only does sound reason direct us to refuse the guidance of those who did or taught anything wrong, but it is incumbent on the lover of truth, by

all means, and if death be threatened, even before his own life,
to choose to do and say what is right.

— *First Apology* 2[28]

Justin knew that most people simply followed what their fathers believed, not investigating for themselves the truth of the claims. This laid a heavy burden upon the Christian apologist to show the wisdom in abandoning such ancient beliefs for the "new" faith of Christianity.

It was in a similar climate that Matthew wrote his Gospel, about a century before Justin, so he wanted to emphasize the family roots of Jesus to his primarily Jewish readers and show the Roman Empire that Christianity was no new religion — through its Jewish roots, it dates back to the time of the patriarchs. Thus, he announces his Gospel with a genealogy of Jesus, beginning with Abraham: "The book of the genealogy of Jesus Christ, the son of David, the son of Abraham" (Mt 1:1). Jesus is part of the great and ancient family of Israel and a continuation of a faith that spans centuries. He is the fulfillment of venerable beliefs. What to a modern reader appears to be an inconsequential family tree is, for Matthew's first readers, an important connection between their new faith and the faith of previous generations.

Matthew goes beyond just saying that Jesus is part of the family of Israel, however; he also proclaims specifically that Jesus is the "son of Abraham," evoking the image of Isaac, the son of Abraham by his wife, Sarah. And this is no surprise. Christians throughout history have noticed the deep connections between Isaac and Christ; of all the types of Christ in the Old Testament, Isaac is the strongest foreshadowing of the person and mission of Christ. In addition to the fact that both Isaac and Christ are the result of a miraculous conception, the two are also prominently linked in the story of the sacrifice of Isaac, found in Genesis 22. As St. Clement of Alexandria notes:

Isaac is another type too . . . this time of the Lord. He was a son, just as is the Son (he is the son of Abraham; Christ, of God). He was a victim, as was the Lord, but his sacrifice was not consummated, while the Lord's was. All he did was to carry the wood of his sacrifice, just as the Lord bore the wood of the cross. Isaac rejoiced for a mystical reason, to prefigure the joy with which the Lord has filled us, in saving us from destruction through his blood.

— Christ the Educator 1.5.23[29]

In the sacrifice of Isaac, we have the model for the sacrifice of Jesus. Abraham is commanded to go to Moriah, which 2 Chronicles 3:1 identifies as the future location of the temple in Jerusalem. He is to offer his beloved son as a sacrifice to God. When Isaac questions his father about the lamb needed for an offering, Abraham unknowingly gives a prophetic answer: "God will provide himself the lamb for a burnt offering, my son" (Gen 22:8). This prophecy comes to pass in two ways: first, in the thicket, God does provide a ram that Abraham offers; but also, God later provides his own beloved Son as a sacrifice for all men.

The crux of this story is the faith of Abraham. God commands him to slay the child who is the fruit of God's own promise. What could have been going through Abraham's mind during the three-day trip to Mt. Moriah? How could he reconcile the seemingly irreconcilable? The author of the letter to the Hebrews conjectures that Abraham obeyed this terrible command of God because "He considered that God was able to raise men even from the dead" (Heb 11:19a). In doing so, Abraham had a foretaste of the way in which the future son of Abraham would be able to follow the command of God to be sacrificed, and yet still be the means through which God's covenant would be established. Abraham, in his great faith, acknowledged that God has power over everything — even death itself. And it is this faith in God's power over death that forms the seed of the Christian faith, a faith founded on the resurrection of the "son of Abraham" Jesus.

In response to Abraham's faithfulness, God makes this promise to him:

> By myself I have sworn, says the LORD, because you have done this, and have not withheld your son, your only son, I will indeed bless you, and I will multiply your descendants as the stars of heaven and as the sand which is on the seashore. And your descendants shall possess the gate of their enemies, and by your descendants shall all the nations of the earth bless themselves, because you have obeyed my voice.
>
> — Gen 22:16b-18

The blessing that God gives to Abraham is fulfilled in a most complete way through Jesus Christ, the true son of Abraham. Matthew bookends his Gospel with this worldwide blessing: he implicitly evokes it by calling Jesus the "son of Abraham" in the first verse of his Gospel, and he explicitly proclaims it in its final verses:

> Go therefore and make disciples of all nations, baptizing them in the name of the Father and of the Son and of the Holy Spirit, teaching them to observe all that I have commanded you; and lo, I am with you always, to the close of the age.
>
> — Mt 28:19-20

The promises made to Abraham that seemed buried and hidden during the long centuries between Abraham and Jesus have now come to full fruition. With the actual sacrifice of the "son of Abraham" and his being raised from the dead, God extends his blessing on all nations, and Jesus commands his apostles to bring that blessing to all peoples.

And it would be another "son of Abraham" who would first take up this mission to the Gentiles. Paul, "a descendant of Abraham" (Rom 11:1), recognizes clearly that now, through Christ, the promises God made to Abraham have been fulfilled. And he realizes that the means by which people receive this blessing is the very thing that was tested in Abraham: faith.

> And the scripture, foreseeing that God would justify the Gentiles by faith, preached the gospel beforehand to Abraham, saying, "In you shall all the nations be blessed." So then, those who are men of faith are blessed with Abraham who had faith.
>
> — Gal 3:8-9

When God called Abraham to sacrifice his son, he tested Abraham's faith: did Abraham trust that God had the power to overcome even death? Abraham believed, and God saved his son from destruction. Now those who come to God by faith in the one who was sacrificed but overcame death are also saved from destruction. We, too, become the children of Abraham, under the promises given to him:

> But now that faith has come, we are no longer under a custodian; for in Christ Jesus you are all sons of God, through faith. For as many of you as were baptized into Christ have put on Christ. There is neither Jew nor Greek, there is neither slave nor free, there is neither male nor female; for you are all one in Christ Jesus. And if you are Christ's, then you are Abraham's offspring, heirs according to promise.
>
> — Gal 3:25-29

Physical lineage is no longer the means of passing on God's blessing and being part of his family. John the Baptist announces this new way of generation when he condemns the bearers of Abraham's DNA:

> "Do not presume to say to yourselves, 'We have Abraham as our father;' for I tell you, God is able from these stones to raise up children to Abraham. Even now the axe is laid to the root of the trees; every tree therefore that does not bear good fruit is cut down and thrown into the fire."
>
> — Mt 3:9-10

Physical membership in Abraham's family no longer matters in the new family that Jesus inaugurates. Jesus himself announces the new type of family he has created when he states:

> "For whoever does the will of my Father in heaven is my brother, and sister, and mother."
>
> — Mt 12:50

Having faith to do the will of the Father — which is what Abraham had — is now the only means of being in God's family.

If faith is the invitation to be in God's family, then we who desire to be in that family must know of what faith consists. Too often, what we call "faith" is little more than simply an intellectual assent: "I believe that he is telling the truth based on the evidence" or "I believe the sun will rise tomorrow." Thus, "faith" is reduced to what can be perceived by the physical senses, especially the sense of sight.

But actual faith is much more than that, and it is dependent upon a sight deeper than that of the eyes. Faith is complete trust in the promises of another. It is, in a sense, a union between two people: when you have faith in another, you bind yourself to that person and affirm with your whole being that the other person is trustworthy. You are willing to risk yourself in that belief. Ultimately, faith and trust are two sides of the same coin: without one, you cannot have the other. This is why betrayal of trust is so harmful.

To have faith in Christ, then, is to give complete assent — body, mind, and soul — in trust to him. We bind our fate to his and by doing so, we share in Christ's fate — glorification. St. Paul writes:

> Christ has been raised from the dead, the first fruits of those who have fallen asleep. For as by a man came death, by a man has come also the resurrection of the dead. For as in Adam all die, so also in Christ shall all be made alive. But each in his

own order: Christ the first fruits, then at his coming those who belong to Christ.

— 1 Cor 15:20-21

Christ was the first faithful son of the Father, offering himself as a sacrifice for man's sins. In return, God gave him glory beyond glory. One who has faith in Christ's salvific death — binding his whole person to that event — will one day also be glorified with him.

This glorification is part of God's plan of salvation, dating back to the most ancient of times. The promises he made to Abraham many millennia ago were fulfilled in Christ and are actualized in the Church. Beginning with the seed of Abraham, God has been working on our salvation, allowing it to find root in Christ and flower in us. We who follow Christ can be confident that our faith did not originate with the Nazarene carpenter, but instead began centuries before that, in a man willing to put his trust in God when it made no sense. We, too, are called to that faith, knowing that God will hold nothing back to save us — not even his beloved Son.

REFERENCES

Mt 1:1

For Reflection

- If faith is a way of seeing, do I look for God's activity in my life?
- Do I see him with love and gratitude in all that each day brings?

SON

Son of David

"What do you think of the Christ? Whose son is he?"
"The son of David."

In 1925, the world found itself in deep unrest. During the pause between the great World Wars, it was clear that the precarious peace that existed between the nations could not last. Surely, conflict would come again, plunging the world deeper into misery. In response to this anxiety, Pope Pius XI instituted a new liturgical feast, one that would proclaim Jesus as the true ruler of all, Christ the King. he wrote:

> We remember saying that these manifold evils in the world were due to the fact that the majority of men had thrust Jesus Christ and his holy law out of their lives; that these had no place either in private affairs or in politics: and . . . that as long as individuals and states refused to submit to the rule of our Savior, there would be no really hopeful prospect of a lasting peace among nations.
>
> *— Quas Primas* 1 [30]

Without Christ as King, the world must devolve into misery and chaos, and it is only when he is proclaimed as the ruler over all that peace can come into the world.

Many centuries before, our evangelist Matthew also recognized the importance of proclaiming the kingship of Christ. He does so in many ways in his Gospel, assigning to Jesus titles like "King of Israel" and "King of the Jews." But it is Matthew's linking of Jesus to the great king David that most clearly declares Christ's kingship.

He establishes this connection at the very beginning of his Gospel, when he mentions forty ancestors in Christ's genealogy — but only one is given a title. In verse 6, Matthew lists "Jesse the father of David the king." Although many of the men on the list following David were also kings, only David is labeled as such. David is the king *par excellence* in the Old Testament; none of the other Israelite kings comes close to his greatness. He is the model that will be superseded only with the coming of the Messiah.

It is Matthew's contention that with Jesus, the "son of David" (Mt 1:1), Israel finally has a new Davidic king who, as the Messiah, not only meets the standard set by the son of Jesse but exceeds it. Christ is the new king of Israel ruling on David's throne. The events of Palm Sunday emphasize that role and show that Christ himself wished to proclaim this kingship of his to the people. In the days leading up to his crucifixion, Christ chooses to ride into the royal city of Jerusalem on an ass, which Matthew notes as the fulfillment of a prophecy:

> And when they drew near to Jerusalem and came to Bethphage, to the Mount of Olives, then Jesus sent two disciples, saying to them, "Go into the village opposite you, and immediately you will find an ass tied, and a colt with her; untie them and bring them to me. If any one says anything to you, you shall say, 'The Lord has need of them,' and he will send them immediately." This took place to fulfill what was spoken by the prophet, saying, "Tell the daughter of Zion, Behold, your king is coming to you, humble, and mounted on an ass, and on a colt, the foal of an ass."
>
> — Mt 21:1-5

At the beginning of the final week before his death and resurrection, Jesus presents himself as the new king of Israel. The people crowding the streets of Jerusalem understand the allusion when they proclaim in response, "Hosanna to the Son of David! Blessed is he who comes in the name of the Lord! Hosanna in the highest!" (Mt 21:9). The longing for a son of David to come as the Messiah was deeply ingrained in the psyche of the Jewish people of Jesus' time, originating in Nathan's prophecy to David:

> "When your days are fulfilled and you lie down with your fathers, I will raise up your offspring after you, who shall come forth from your body, and I will establish his kingdom. He shall build a house for my name, and I will establish the throne of his kingdom for ever. I will be his father, and he shall be my son."
>
> — 2 Sam 7:12-14a

The coming Messianic Davidic King was looked upon as someone who would crush Israel's political enemies and establish the Chosen People as the rulers of the world. One Jewish document from shortly before the time of Christ declares:

> Behold, O Lord, and raise up unto them their king, the son of David, At the time in which you see, O God, may he reign over Israel your servant and gird him with strength, that he may shatter unrighteous rulers, and that he may purge Jerusalem from nations that trample [her] down to destruction. Wisely, righteously he shall thrust out sinners from [the] inheritance, he shall destroy the pride of the sinner as a potter's vessel. With a rod of iron he shall break in pieces all their substance, He shall destroy the godless nations with the word of his mouth; At his rebuke nations shall flee before him, And he shall reprove sinners for the thoughts of their heart.
>
> — *Psalm of Solomon* 17[31]

This passage reflects the deep integration of political and religious aspirations for the ancient Jew — the coming of the Messiah was as much a political event as a religious one. It would entail the restoration of the nation of Israel and the destruction of alien nations. It would be the vindication of the true God and would inaugurate an era when true worship could at long last commence.

Although the Church has always proclaimed the kingship of Christ over all peoples and all nations, this kingship is not an outwardly political one, as the Jews at the time of Jesus assumed of the coming Messiah. No, his kingship means that he reigns over the hearts of men, and it is given to Christ not because of anything he does but because of who he is. In the fifth century, St. Cyril of Alexandria declared:

> Christ has dominion over all creatures, a dominion not seized by violence nor usurped, but his by essence and by nature.[32]

As God, he reigns over all of creation; as man, he is the rightful owner of kingship over all men. But in his great love for us, Christ also acquires kingship through his salvific actions. In his encyclical instituting the feast of Christ the King, Pope Pius XI writes:

> His kingship is founded upon the ineffable hypostatic union [of his divine and human natures]. From this it follows not only that Christ is to be adored by angels and men, but that to him as man angels and men are subject, and must recognize his empire; by reason of the hypostatic union Christ has power over all creatures. But a thought that must give us even greater joy and consolation is this that Christ is our King by acquired, as well as by natural right, for he is our Redeemer. Would that they who forget what they have cost their Savior might recall the words: "You were not redeemed with corruptible things, but with the precious blood of Christ, as of a lamb unspotted and undefiled." We are no longer our own property, for Christ has purchased us "with a great price"; our very bodies are the "members of Christ."
>
> — *Quas Primas* 13[33]

But although Christ's kingship is not outwardly political, it does have political ramifications — as Pope Pius understood. Those rulers who allow Christ to reign in their hearts will rule differently than those who do not, understanding the inherent dignity of all men and women and striving to protect that dignity through their policies, with far-reaching consequences in the political affairs of the nations.

But the kingdom of Christ extends beyond the political sphere. Christ, by both his nature and his work, has authority over all creation; this authority as son of David extends even over disease and the powers of hell. Three times in the Gospel of Matthew, Jesus is addressed as the "son of David" in the context of a petition. What is striking is the common theme of the requests. First, two blind men approach Jesus and cry out, "Have mercy on us, Son of David" (Mt 9:27). Later, a Canaanite woman whose daughter was possessed by a demon calls out to him, "Have mercy on me, O Lord, Son of David" (Mt 15:22). Then finally, two more blind men beg him, "Have mercy on us, Son of David!" (Mt 20:30). Each time, the supplicant appeals to the mercy of Jesus.

Behind these appeals must be belief in Christ's authority, for he can only be merciful if he has the power to do something to help. The exercise of mercy is a vital component of kingship: a king sees the misfortune of those under his rule and takes pity on them. And the greatest of kings, David, was the epitome of mercy: when Saul, who was attempting to kill young David without justification, was delivered into the future king's hands, David stayed his hand, granting mercy to his enemy instead of justice (1 Sam 26:5-10). As the kingly son of David, Jesus has the authority to grant mercy to others, and the desire to pour out this mercy as did David. It is to this mercy that these people who call him Son of David are appealing. They wish him to exercise his kingly authority over disease and demonic powers for their benefit. And in each case, Jesus does so.

Jesus, therefore, is understood by those around him as claiming the royal throne of David, and many of the people accept him as the rightful heir to that throne. Yet many of those who proclaimed

"Hosanna to the Son of David!" had a limited understanding of the role to be played by this Son of David; they wished him to be a political or military leader. So Jesus seeks to reveal the true identity of the Messianic Son of David:

> Now while the Pharisees were gathered together, Jesus asked them a question, saying, "What do you think of the Christ? Whose son is he?" They said to him, "The son of David." He said to them, "How is it then that David, inspired by the Spirit, calls him Lord, saying, 'The Lord said to my Lord, Sit at my right hand, till I put thy enemies under thy feet'? If David thus calls him Lord, how is he his son?"

— Mt 22:41-45

Jesus is quoting Psalm 110, a messianic Psalm beloved by the first-century Church. In fact, it is the most used Old Testament text in all of the New Testament.

This discussion with the Pharisees occurs shortly before the events of Holy Week, and Jesus is urging all who will listen to comprehend the mystery of his person. He does this by explaining the meaning of the Scriptures about himself. Before Jesus begins his interpretation, though, he establishes the authority of this text by noting its dual authorship: "How is it then that David, inspired by the Spirit . . ." According to Christ, David is the one speaking in this Psalm, but his words are beyond his own ability — they are inspired by God himself. This is a hint to his listeners that they, too, must be open to the Spirit in order to understand the Christ's true identity.

Jesus cites David's first line, "The Lord said to my Lord," which poses a problem: if the first "Lord" is clearly God himself, who is the second? Most scribes would say that it is the Messiah; who else could David call "Lord" other than God and the Messiah? Yet the Messiah is also David's "son," and in the Jewish culture, a father would never call his son "Lord." So why is the Messiah deserving of the title "Lord" even from his "father" David?

Jesus does not answer this question explicitly, wishing his listeners to come to comprehension on their own. They need to see that the Christ is not simply a king who receives his power due to his Davidic bloodlines; he is King due to his divine sonship. While remaining strictly monotheistic, this psalm assigns to the Messiah divine prerogatives such as "executing judgment among the nations" (v. 6). Jesus is impressing upon his followers that the status of the coming Messiah is so great that he is equal to God. St. Augustine, meditating on this passage, writes:

> Thus you have heard that Christ is both David's Son and David's Lord:
>
> David's Lord always, David's Son in time.
>
> David's Lord, born of the substance of his Father;
>
> David's Son, born of the Virgin Mary, conceived by the Holy Spirit.
>
> Let us hold fast both. The one of them will be our eternal habitation; the other is our deliverance from our present exile.
>
> — *Sermon* 92.3[34]

The application of this psalm to Jesus is so powerful that the Church prays it every Sunday evening in the Liturgy of the Hours, along with a Christological canticle from the New Testament. The Church, then, each time Christ's resurrection is celebrated, prays within the reality that the Messiah, as the son of David, is the true king who rules, while the enemies of man — sin and death — are put under his feet. As the Davidic King, he is merciful to all who are still ruled by these enemies, freeing them from slavery to sin and death and making them a part of his everlasting kingdom.

REFERENCES

Mt 1:1, 9:27, 12:23, 15:22, 20:30-31, 21:9-15, 22:41-46

For Reflection

- Do I allow the Lord to reign in my relationships, vocation, work, and leisure time?
- Does it change how I vote, how I work, and how I love?

Son of Man

"For the Son of Man is going to come in his
Father's glory with his angels."

Everyone loves a good mystery. Tantalizing clues throughout the story lead the reader to speculate on the outcome, yet don't give away the ending. The well-written mystery will also contain red herrings, directing the reader down alternative paths to keep him guessing. If you can deduce the ending before it is revealed, so much the better. Once the plot has reached its climax, it's fun to go back and review the author's clues to see how they subtly direct the reader to the true conclusion.

When it comes to the story of Jesus, there is one mystery whose resolution still eludes both scholars and saints: Christ's reference to himself with the enigmatic title "Son of Man." In all the Gospels, only Jesus uses this title, and this singular usage has given it even greater import. His followers, however, have never seen fit to use it themselves as a title for Christ. One would think that the term for himself that Jesus was most fond of would be widely used among Christians, but the opposite is true. Perhaps Jesus intended that the title be mysterious. Had he referred to himself with more common Christological titles such as "Son of David" or "Christ" or "Son of God," his hearers would have believed that they fully grasped him and his mission — although in what would have most likely been an incomplete way. A title such as "Son of David" would have conjured up images of a military commander crushing his enemies through strength of arms. Few would have understood the necessity for suffering from the "Christ." And a title like "Son of

God" would have surely led to a diminishment of the importance of Jesus' true humanity.

So Jesus used the title "Son of Man" to refer to himself, a title with a history not usually associated with the coming Messiah. What then did he mean by this title? No one fully knows; here is one mystery whose resolution will not be completely unveiled this side of heaven. But this is as it should be, for if we believe we understand all there is to know about Jesus, we would have a poor understanding indeed. Saints and scholars have studied the life and work of Jesus Christ for centuries, but in truth have only scratched the surface of the reality that is the God-man. Shortly before he died, St. Thomas Aquinas, the greatest theologian of the Church and author of voluminous theological and philosophical works, had a mystical experience during Mass which led him to declare that "such secrets have been revealed to me that all I have written now appears of little value." St. Thomas realized that we here on earth can only begin to understand who Jesus is. The true meaning of the title "Son of Man" will likely be something we never fully comprehend.

Of all the possible meanings of "Son of Man," it is most obviously a reference to Christ's true humanity. He is truly born into the human race, taking on human flesh. He does not simply appear to be human, acting the part for those around him. No, he is a man in all things except sin; he laughs, he cries, he enjoys the company of friends and is hurt at their betrayal. By becoming man, God does not simply lift man out of the human condition but, indeed, takes it on and sanctifies it. All labor, recreation, and other human activities become part of the path to holiness and salvation.

As the Fathers liked to say, "What he did not assume he did not redeem." The truth of the Incarnation is fundamental to Christianity and can never be overemphasized. It was a man who caused the fall of the human race and a man is required to redeem it. Every action of Christ's — his birth to Mary, nursing at her breast, playing with his childhood friends, learning his trade from Joseph, studying the Torah — are part of the plan of salvation, and those same daily tasks — work, study, play — become the path to salvation for his followers.

Jesus said:

> "The Son of man came eating and drinking, and they say, 'Behold, a glutton and a drunkard, a friend of tax collectors and sinners!'"
>
> — Mt 11:19

Jesus ate and drank like any man; he was even accused of being a drunkard! His life was the life of a real man; he didn't simply go through the motions leading up to his public ministry and Passion. In order to redeem the life of man, he became an ordinary man.

However, there is more to the term "Son of Man" than simply a declaration of membership in the human race. Jesus' use of this title hearkens back to the Old Testament, where the title "Son of Man" is primarily used in two places in the ancient texts: the writings of the prophets Ezekiel and Daniel. Ezekiel writes:

> When I saw [the likeness of the glory of the LORD], I fell upon my face, and I heard the voice of one speaking. And he said to me, "Son of man, stand upon your feet, and I will speak with you."
>
> — Ezek 2:1

So by using this title, the Lord indicates the humility and the smallness of man in comparison to the Almighty God. Ezekiel, a "son of man," is nothing compared to the Lord of Hosts. Although man is the greatest creation, he is insignificant in relation to the Creator.

In Daniel, on the other hand, the phrase is used in a much different light. There, Daniel clearly uses it to indicate a Messianic figure in glory:

> I saw in the night visions, and behold, with the clouds of heaven there came one like a son of man, and he came to the Ancient of Days and was presented before him. And to him was given dominion and glory and kingdom, that all peoples, nations, and languages should serve him; his dominion is an everlasting dominion, which shall not pass away, and his kingdom one that shall not be destroyed.
>
> — Dan 7:13-14

This "son of man" is a figure of great prominence, given immense authority and majesty. No one surpasses him in the glory that is bestowed upon him.

Thus, the two connotations of the title "Son of Man" in the Old Testament are the humility of man and the glorification that awaits him. This dual nature of humility/glory continues in Matthew's Gospel. Overwhelmingly, in Matthew, Jesus uses the term "Son of Man" in one of two contexts: the humiliating suffering that he must endure, or his glorious second coming. In Matthew 20:18-19, for instance, Jesus predicts:

> "Behold, we are going up to Jerusalem; and the Son of man will be delivered to the chief priests and scribes, and they will condemn him to death, and deliver him to the Gentiles to be mocked and scourged and crucified, and he will be raised on the third day."

It is the Son of Man who will be delivered unto death for his fellow man. But Jesus also proclaims:

> "When the Son of man comes in his glory, and all the angels with him, then he will sit on his glorious throne."
>
> — Mt 25:31

The suffering of the Son of Man, though necessary, is not the final word; through this suffering he will be vindicated. And, as Daniel foresaw, he will be "given dominion and glory and kingdom."

The title "Son of Man," therefore, speaks to the extremes of Jesus' life and mission: from the very depths of human misery he experienced in his Passion to his exaltation as the Ruler of the Universe. These two extremes, however, are not to be separated; they are intimately united in Christ's mission.

We see this as well in the account of the Transfiguration. After seeing Elijah and Moses confer with Jesus, and seeing Jesus transfigured and receiving the blessing of the Father as his Son, the three apostles are told to "tell no one the vision, until *the Son of man is raised from the dead.*" The apostles do not understand what this means. They ask, "Then why do the scribes say that first Eli'jah must come?" Jesus replies:

> "Elijah does come, and he is to restore all things; but I tell you that Elijah has already come, and they did not know him, but did to him whatever they pleased. So also *the Son of man will suffer at their hands.*"
>
> — Mt 17:9-12 (emphasis added)

So even in the very hour when Jesus is glorified by the Father, he still points to the suffering he must endure. In the mystery of Jesus, the glory he receives from the Father comes by way of his humility.

Throughout Jesus' public ministry, the apostles struggle to grasp the dual aspects of his mission. They anticipate Christ's glory without understanding the price he would have to pay for it. On the road to Jerusalem, when Jesus predicts to his apostles the Son of Man's death by crucifixion (Mt 20:17-19), it leads to a dispute among them — not about the suffering they would also endure, but about who would sit on his right and left in his kingdom! The mother of Zebedee's sons desires these seats for James and John, not realizing their price. Jesus immediately directs their attention to the suffering that is a part of being in his kingdom:

> "You do not know what you are asking. Are you able to drink the cup that I am to drink?"
>
> —Mt 20:22

Those who would sit with him in glory must drink the cup of his suffering.

After the resurrection, however, led by the Holy Spirit, the followers of Christ do begin to comprehend the necessity of suffering to achieve glorification — a path many of them would end up imitating in their own lives. The first martyr, Stephen, is the first example of this pattern, conforming completely to Christ's passion during his own martyrdom. Stephen quotes the passage from Daniel above as he has a vision of the glorified Christ:

> But [Stephen], full of the Holy Spirit, gazed into heaven and saw the glory of God, and Jesus standing at the right hand of God; and he said, "Behold, I see the heavens opened, and the Son of man standing at the right hand of God."
>
> — Acts 7:55-56

Stephen, by his very life, imitates that of his Master.

St. Paul, who witnessed this event as a persecutor of the Church, would eventually come to grasp the importance of lowering oneself in order to be raised. He captures this movement from humility to glory in his moving piece in the letter to the Philippians:

> Have this mind among you, which was in Christ Jesus, who, though he was in the form of God, did not consider equality with God a thing to be grasped, but emptied himself, taking the form of a servant, being born in the likeness of men. And being found in human form he humbled himself and became obedient unto death, even death on a cross. Therefore God has highly exalted him and bestowed on him the name which is above every name, that at the name of Jesus every knee should bow, in heaven and on earth and under the earth, and every tongue confess that Jesus Christ is Lord, to the glory of God the Father.
>
> — Phil 2:5-11

The "Son of Man" willingly debases himself, opening himself up to betrayal and suffering, and in doing so, is glorified by his Father.

One model of the self-abasement needed to follow Christ is St. Thérèse of Lisieux, the Little Flower. Although her heart's desire was to be a great missionary, she came to realize that her path to holiness would instead entail doing "little" acts for God. She sacrificed her missionary desires and offered her humble life as a nun entirely to God, lived a simple life, and died at the age of twenty-four in a convent in France. By all worldly accounts, she had no impact on the world and was inconsequential in every way. Yet God exalted her, allowing her intercession from heaven to be so powerful that she became one of the most beloved saints of our times. After her death, she became the Church's patroness of missions and, through her heavenly intercession, has converted hearts throughout the world.

"The Son of man came not to be served but to serve, and to give his life as a ransom for many" (Mt 20:28). All who desire to follow Christ will have to do likewise. Most of us will not do great things and will have little noticeable impact on the world in which we live. Yet, everyone can do little things with great love. By making daily sacrifices for others, we humble ourselves and imitate the Lord.

Christ did not just humble himself during his Passion — he did it on a daily basis during the thirty years he spent as an ordinary Nazarene. Here was the One who made heaven and earth, having to use common tools to make a table! The One who keeps all things in existence, having to eat and drink in order to stay alive! In those "hidden years," we can see a model for each of us: every task and duty we perform can be united to Christ and offered to the Father for our own salvation and the salvation of others. And, as God glorified Christ, in the life to come he will most surely glorify those who follow his humble path, uniting them to Christ in the kingdom that shall not be destroyed.

REFERENCES

Mt 8:20, 9:6, 10:23, 11:19, 12:8, 12:32, 12:40, 13:37-41, 16:13, 16:27-28, 17:9-12, 17:22, 19:28, 20:18, 20:28, 24:27, 24:30, 24:37, 24:39, 24:44, 25:31, 26:2, 26:24, 26:45, 26:64

For Reflection

- Do I see "smallness" as a path to holiness?
- Do I let the little indignities of life draw me closer to God, or do they make me bitter and resentful?

Son of God

"This was not revealed to you by man, but by my
Father in heaven."

We find in the Gospels a host of minor characters who make an
appearance, then quickly fade into obscurity. Simon of Cyrene,
Nicodemus, Joseph of Arimathea, and blind Bartimaeus all
enter the story of Christ's life in a dramatic way, but then largely
disappear. Each has a role to play in the unfolding mission of the
Redeemer, but we wish we could know more about how such
person's encounters with Christ impacted the rest of their lives.
Did Simon become a member of the early Church? Did Nicodemus
leave the ranks of the Pharisees to become an apostle of the Risen
Lord? Surely they were transformed in some way, and it will be one
of the joys of heaven to find out how.

In Matthew's Gospel there is a minor character — not even
named — who, during the crucifixion, announces the climatic
declaration of the entire Gospel:

> And behold, the curtain of the temple was torn in two, from
> top to bottom; and the earth shook, and the rocks were split;
> the tombs also were opened, and many bodies of the saints
> who had fallen asleep were raised, and coming out of the tombs
> after his resurrection they went into the holy city and appeared
> to many. When the centurion and those who were with him,
> keeping watch over Jesus, saw the earthquake and what took
> place, they were filled with awe, and said, "Truly this was the
> Son of God!"

— Mt 27:51-54

Tradition tells us that this Roman centurion — who gives voice to the underlying message Matthew is intent on conveying: that Jesus is, indeed, the Son of God — was named Longinus, and that he was also the one who pierced the side of Christ (cf. Jn 19:34), causing blood and water to flow out from it. Tradition further relates that Longinus' eyes had been afflicted and were instantly healed when the blood and water from Christ's side touched them. After this encounter, he converted to the Christian faith, was baptized, left the army, and was eventually martyred. Both the Catholic and Orthodox Churches now honor him as a saint. St. Longinus' confession at the cross — that Jesus was the "Son of God" — completely changed his life forever.

The title "Son of God" is used not only by those who are transformed by Christ, but it's also on the lips of his enemies — Satan first, and then the chief priests — when they question him. But, most importantly, it forms the core of the Christian confession of faith regarding the identity of Jesus of Nazareth, a confession possible only by supernatural intervention. St. Longinus' confession becomes the ultimate confession used by Matthew to announce that the fears of Christ's enemies are true: Jesus of Nazareth is the Son of God.

The first reference to this title in Matthew occurs during the episode of the temptation in the desert found in Chapter 4. Satan is preparing to do battle with Jesus and he wants to know everything he can about his adversary. Whom, exactly, is he dealing with? Is this merely a man — a special one, possibly, but a man, nonetheless — or is he something more?

If he is a man, there is always the simple solution of death if he gets in the way. The initial inquiry from Satan to Jesus is, "If you are the Son of God, tell these stones to become bread" (Mt 4:3). After Jesus successfully parries this first thrust, Satan again alludes to Jesus' origins during the next temptation:

"If you are the Son of God, throw yourself down; for it is written, 'He will give his angels charge of you,' and 'On their hands they will bear you up, lest you strike your foot against a stone.'"

— Mt 4:6

Satan assumes that the identity "Son of God" conveys great power and a unique relationship with God. He knows that if this Jesus is really the Son of God, he will have to deal with him in a wholly different manner than if he were a simple prophet or teacher. Christ's refusal to succumb to Satan's first two temptations must tell Satan something significant, for in the third temptation, he no longer asks Jesus if he is the Son of God:

The devil took him to a very high mountain, and showed him all the kingdoms of the world and the glory of them; and he said to him, "All these I will give you, if you will fall down and worship me."

— Mt 4:9

Satan recognizes, at least to some extent, the reality of the person standing before him — and thus, he must make a radical attempt to prevent him from completing his mission. Satan was successful in tempting Adam and Eve with the promise to be "like God," but with Jesus, he sees that he must push harder and promise everything in his power to give. Of course, Jesus resists this temptation. As the divine Son, he will justly receive all of this, if he fulfills the will of the Father.

Satan is not the only one curious about Jesus' origins, however. During the trial before the crucifixion, the high priest is anxious to learn the true identity of the man who is accused of such blasphemous deeds:

"I charge you under oath by the living God: Tell us if you are the Christ, the Son of God."

— Mt 26:63

Later, while Jesus is hanging on the cross, people in the crowd cry out, "If you are the Son of God, come down from the cross" (Mt 27:40). Even at the moment of Jesus' apparent defeat, his enemies are not completely confident in their skepticism. Might there be a hopeful note in their accusations? They, like all Jews, wanted God to set up his Kingdom here on earth. They were truly expecting the Messiah to come. But they simply could not see how this humble carpenter from Galilee could be part of that plan, so they give him a final opportunity to prove himself: surely, if he is really the Messiah, if he is the Son of God, he will be able to overcome those who oppose him! His apparent failure to do so confirms their decision to reject him. Unable to see any other way to proceed, they move forward with their solution: *crucify* him! His death will surely be the end of his mission.

While Christ's enemies question his identity, two confessions in Matthew's Gospel highlight the truth of Jesus' divine sonship: those of Peter and Longinus. Peter's famous confession — "You are the Christ, the Son of the living God" (Mt 16:16) — is immediately followed by Jesus' revelation of its heavenly origin:

> "Blessed are you, Simon son of Jonah, for this was not revealed to you by man, *but by my Father in heaven.*"
>
> — Mt 16:17, emphasis added

Here, Jesus makes a significant point. Peter did not come to the conclusion that Jesus was the Son of God by intellectual reasoning. No, his belief was a gift from God, a penetration of heavenly wisdom into Peter's mind. Our ability to reason can be a powerful faculty — but it is only capable of processing what the senses perceive, and the truth of the divinity of Christ transcends such ability. It had to be revealed by God himself to Peter, as it must be for all believers. And this confession is life-changing:

> Whoever confesses that Jesus is the Son of God, God abides in him, and he in God.
>
> — 1 Jn 4:15

At churches around the world each Sunday, Christians confess that Jesus Christ is "the only Son of God, eternally begotten of the Father, God from God, Light from Light, true God from true God, begotten, not made, one in Being with the Father." Although originally forged in the fires of controversy, seventeen centuries later, the power of these words can be lost on us. But this language is so radical that only by divine revelation can man truly accept and confess it.

Like any true son, Jesus has received from his Father his father's nature. The son of a man is a man, and the Son of God is God. It took hundreds of years to devise language to explain how the Son and the Father can both be God while there is yet only one God, but the truth of that reality is based on the confessions of men like Peter and Longinus. So, although the term "Son of God" in the Old Testament could sometimes merely represent one on whom God's favor rests, Matthew's careful use of the term reveals more: the true inner identity of Jesus, the fullness of divinity he has received from all time from the Father. He is his "only Son."

Furthermore, the Son is the means by which man can know the Father.

> "No one knows the Father except the Son and any one to whom the Son chooses to reveal him."
>
> — Mt 11:27

It is only through the Son that man is able to access the inaccessible and know the unknowable: the inner life of God. Divinity is so unlike humanity that it is certainly impossible, by human reason alone, to really know God. We can know he exists and understand certain characteristics of his nature by reason — but truly knowing him, not simply knowing about him, is impossible without the revelation of Jesus Christ.

If a person wished to learn about a foreign country, reading and study about that country could eventually tell him a lot about it. But if he really wished to *know* that country, he would have to move there, learn the language, and interact with the locals. Only by immersion into the culture would he truly know it. If he immersed himself long enough, he might eventually become indistinguishable from a native.

This is how it is with knowing God. We can study and read about him and understand parts of his nature. But to truly know him, we must immerse ourselves in Jesus Christ — through prayer, sacraments, and service — and in doing so, we will be transformed more and more into the likeness of Christ.

Sons are often reflections of their fathers, and this is even truer of Jesus. Paul tells us that Christ is the "image of the invisible God" (Col 1:15). As the Son of God, Jesus reflects the Father perfectly, in this way making him known to man.

In Old Testament times, the people of God were forbidden to make any images of the divine; how could man ever represent truly the Lord, who is essentially *Other*? Their revelation of God was incomplete and fragmentary, so any image they made was sure to be deficient in some way. Yet with the coming of Christ, he has been made known. This reality has many implications, including the use of images to reflect God. During the seventh century of the Christian era, some members of the Church began to complain that images of Christ were a violation of this commandment and should be destroyed. Yet the Church, led by St. John of Damascus, proclaimed that images of Christ were wholly appropriate because, through the Incarnation, God had made himself known to man:

> Of old God the incorporeal and uncircumscribed was not depicted at all. But now that God has appeared in the flesh and lived among men, I make an image of the God who can be seen. I do not worship matter but I worship the Creator of matter, who for my sake became material and deigned to dwell in matter, who through matter effected my salvation.
>
> — *On Icons*[35]

God had seen fit to reveal himself in his Son the "image of the invisible God," so images of the divine Son were now worthy of devotion.

The beauty of the Incarnation is that God condescended to make himself known to man in the way we could best know him — as one of us. he didn't have to send his Son, but he desired to be known by his creation. He revealed his nature, a nature that can be described in the single word "love" (cf. 1 Jn 4:8). Love is indescribable, but it can be seen. One simply has to look at Jesus.

For St. Longinus, it was the image of the crucified Jesus that revealed to him the divinity of Christ. That image still represents the clearest picture of the inner life of God, an inner life that pours itself out in love for others. We are called to imitate this life, pouring ourselves out in love for our families, friends, and all whom we encounter. By doing so, we, too, become sons of God.

REFERENCES

Mt 4:3-6, 8:29, 14:33, 16:16, 26:63, 27:40, 27:43, 27:54

For Reflection

- Does my life show that Christianity is more than just an intellectual philosophy?
- Do I recognize that it is a gift from God, and not the work of men?
- Do I let its teachings and life change me completely from within?

"My Beloved Son"

"This is my beloved Son, with whom I am well pleased."

In 2002, Pope John Paul II announced that he was adding a new set of five mysteries to the Rosary. He called these the "Luminous Mysteries," or "Mysteries of Light." Since the original fifteen mysteries of this dearly loved devotion had been set for centuries, this astounded many Catholics. But it did seem to fill a gap in the existing mysteries; they jumped from the finding of the boy Jesus in the temple to his agony in the Garden of Gethsemane the night before his death, skipping Christ's entire public ministry. The Luminous Mysteries, comprised of the Baptism of Christ, the Wedding at Cana, the Proclamation of the Kingdom, the Transfiguration, and the Institution of the Eucharist, highlight the most important three years of human history by proclaiming Christ's mission as the bearer of light to a world darkened by sin and death.

Two of these mysteries in particular — the Baptism of Christ and the Transfiguration — powerfully depict the illumination that comes from the revelation of Christ. These two events have been linked throughout Church history, an association first visible in the accounts Matthew gives of them. Of the Baptism, Matthew writes:

> Then Jesus came from Galilee to the Jordan to John, to be baptized by him. John would have prevented him, saying, "I need to be baptized by you, and do you come to me?" But Jesus answered him, "Let it be so now; for thus it is fitting for us to fulfill all righteousness." Then he consented. And when Jesus

was baptized, he went up immediately from the water, and behold, the heavens were opened and he saw the Spirit of God descending like a dove, and alighting on him; and lo, a voice from heaven, saying, "This is my beloved Son, with whom I am well pleased."

— Mt 3:13-17

Matthew's account of the Transfiguration bears a remarkable similarity to his account of the Baptism:

And after six days Jesus took with him Peter and James and John his brother, and led them up a high mountain apart. And he was transfigured before them, and his face shone like the sun, and his garments became white as light. And behold, there appeared to them Moses and Elijah, talking with him. And Peter said to Jesus, "Lord, it is well that we are here; if you wish, I will make three booths here, one for you and one for Moses and one for Elijah." He was still speaking, when lo, a bright cloud overshadowed them, and a voice from the cloud said, "This is my beloved Son, with whom I am well pleased; listen to him." When the disciples heard this, they fell on their faces, and were filled with awe. But Jesus came and touched them, saying, "Rise, and have no fear." And when they lifted up their eyes, they saw no one but Jesus only.

— Mt 17:1-8

Each account is fundamentally a "theophany," or manifestation of God. In the Gospels, God the Father is mostly silent; since Jesus, the Son of God, fully reveals the Father, what need is there for the Father to speak? Yet at these two times in Matthew's Gospel, he does speak, each time proclaiming the deep mystery of Christ's identity: this is his "beloved Son," a revelation that is a light cutting into the darkness. Without this divine disclosure, our sin-darkened world would never be able to perceive the divine glory of Jesus, the Son of God. The Father in his loving condescension wants to leave no doubt about whom it is that he sent: his only Son, his *beloved* Son.

Why does the Father specifically call Jesus "beloved"? This

term brings to mind what God told Abraham many centuries before:

> "Take your son, your only son Isaac, *whom you love,* and go to the land of Moriah, and offer him there as a burnt offering upon one of the mountains of which I shall tell you."
>
> — Gen 22:2

God asked Abraham to sacrifice his beloved son in a test of faith; then, in the end, saved Isaac from destruction. However, God's own "beloved" Son will be granted no such reprieve — he will have to be sacrificed on the altar of Calvary to effect our redemption. In calling Jesus his "beloved" Son, the Father is reminding us of the lengths he will go to in order to save fallen humanity: even the one most precious to him will be given over for love of those who have rejected him.

At both the Baptism of Christ and his Transfiguration, Jesus is declared the Father's "beloved Son." However, in the account of the Transfiguration, the Father also adds, "Listen to him." The context of the two events reveals why the Father said this only on the mountain, and not at the Jordan. The revelation at the Baptism was to announce to the whole world that her savior had arrived: the very Son of God had been sent by God to save us. At the Transfiguration, however, only Christ's closest apostles were present. The Father was telling them specifically to listen to his Son and follow him, because they would be the ones who would announce salvation to the ends of the earth.

As we can see countless times throughout the Scriptures, God works out his plan of salvation through his people. He depends upon his followers — such as Peter, James, and John — to extend the work of his beloved Son to all peoples. The apostles were the first to "listen to him," teaching others what they had been taught at the feet of Christ. This process continues with each generation, as new disciples of Christ listen to his words and put them into practice.

Revelation is, by its very nature, an illumination. Left to our own abilities, we are stuck in darkness and ignorance. But when the love of God penetrates our hearts and minds, our understanding of him and his Son is illuminated.

The Christian East pays particular attention to the importance of illumination in the path to holiness. While Western saints who are especially advanced in holiness often display some aspect of Christ's Passion (such as the stigmata of St. Francis of Assisi), in the East, great saints frequently display the reality of the Transfiguration: as they become more and more beloved children of the Father, their very countenance is transfigured, as Christ was transfigured on the mountain. A heavenly glow, the aura of holiness, surrounds them. In fact, many Eastern spiritual fathers describe salvation as a process of transfiguration into the likeness of God.

The Baptism and Transfiguration also teach us a great deal about the inner life of God. Many artistic representations of Christ's Baptism, in both the East and the West, include three angelic figures observing the scene. These figures recall the three visitors who appear to Abraham at Mamre (cf. Gen 18). Tradition has it that the three angels prefigure the Trinity; for example, Rublev's famous icon of this event is titled "The Trinity" (though often called the "hospitality of Abraham"). The reason for the three's inclusion in the renderings of the Baptism is that this event is the first explicit revelation of the Trinity. The Baptism, along with the Transfiguration, reveal that God is not alone, but is a communion of three persons. St. Augustine writes about the Biblical passage on the Baptism:

> Here then we have the Trinity presented in a clear way: the Father in the voice, the Son in the man, the Holy Spirit in the dove. . . . The Lord Christ himself, who comes in the form of a servant to John, is undoubtedly the Son, for here no one can mistake him for either the Father or the Holy Spirit. It is the Son

who comes. And who could have any doubt about the identity of the dove? The Gospel itself most plainly testifies: "The Holy Spirit descended upon him in the form of a dove." So also there can be no doubt whose voice it is who speaks so personally: "You are my beloved Son." So we have the Trinity distinguished.

— Sermon 2:1-2[36]

This is the revelation that is unique to Christianity. Of all the monotheistic religions, only Christianity proclaims that God is not One, but Three. The apostle John was present at both events of illumination, and he sums up the reality of what he was shown in one simple phrase: "God is love." And what is love without a communion that allows its exchange? In an ineffable way, God can be described truly in one word, *love*, even though he cannot be completely grasped even in all the volumes upon volumes of mystical and theological works written about him. This naturally leads us to ask: what, then, makes up love?

St. Augustine taught that love has three components: (1) the lover, (2) the beloved, and (3) the love between the two. We see this perfectly in the Trinity. Jesus is the Father's beloved Son. The Father loves the Son eternally, pouring out his very being, all that he is, in a great and never-ending act of self-gift to the Son. The Son, being the recipient of this love and the image of the Father, returns this infinite love back to him. This love, being the very essence of the Father and the Son, is so complete that it eternally forms another divine person, the Holy Spirit — the bond of love between Father and Son.

God is not alone, a stern and aloof figure who stands apart from all reality. The Christian faith instead proclaims that God is a *family*, as Pope John Paul II once declared:

God in His deepest mystery is not a solitude, but a family, since He has in himself fatherhood, sonship, and the essence of the family, which is love.[37]

If, as Christians, we worship a God who is a loving family, then it is the mission of every Christian family to model itself on the self-giving family of the Trinity. The reality of God as a family — a communion of persons — also means that each person created in the image of God is actually an image of a communion. Man is not a solitary entity whose interactions with others are an optional part of life. Instead, man is fundamentally communal; his very being is dependent upon his relation to others.

The Our Father, the prayer given to us by Christ himself, testifies to the truth of our communal nature — as St. Cyprian, who wrote the first major commentary on this prayer in the third century, says:

> Before all things, the Teacher of peace and the Master of unity would not have prayer to be made singly and individually, as for one who prays to pray for himself alone. For we say not "My Father, which art in heaven," nor "Give me this day my daily bread;" nor does each one ask that only his own debt should be forgiven him; nor does he request for himself alone that he may not be led into temptation, and delivered from evil. Our prayer is public and common; and when we pray, we pray not for one, but for the whole people, because we the whole people are one.
>
> — *On the Lord's Prayer* 8[38]

Our individual relationship with God is not the entirety of our bond with him. God relates to us as a body — specifically, the Body of Christ. One of the Fathers' common images for the Church is that of the ark: just as only those joined with Noah in his boat could be saved from the destructive waters, so, too, only those joined with Christ in his Church are able to obtain salvation. Each person is brought to salvation not as an individual, but as a member of the larger body of the Church, a passenger on the ark. For all of eternity, the saints will worship God united as one, while still being distinct from each other — just as God is united in one nature, yet distinct in three persons.

Modern society, however, rejects the beauty of our communal nature in favor of a devotion to individualism that approaches the religious, giving birth to the cynical saying that "hell is other people." Yet if we are created in the Trinitarian image of God, then hell actually consists of being absolutely, completely alone — cut off from God and from others. Hell is "the suffering of being no longer able to love," cries Elder Zosima in *The Brothers Karamazov*. There is no greater deformation of the human person than to be so alone, for without communion, we have no one to love. Being utterly alone, man is unable to do what he was created to do.

The revelation that Jesus is God's beloved Son, then, sheds light not only on his identity, but on man's identity as well. We are made for others — for God first, but for our fellow man as well. The root of all sin is selfishness, since it rejects the inner truth of the nature of man. That nature is revealed in this exchange between Jesus and a lawyer:

> And behold, a lawyer stood up to put him to the test, saying, "Teacher, what shall I do to inherit eternal life?" He said to him, "What is written in the law? How do you read?" And he answered, "You shall love the Lord your God with all your heart, and with all your soul, and with all your strength, and with all your mind; and your neighbor as yourself." And he said to him, "You have answered right; do this, and you will live."
>
> — Lk 10:25-27

To inherit eternal life — to fulfill the destiny God has intended for each of us — we are called to love God and love others. This is the fulfillment of the communal nature imbedded in the heart of man, leading to an eternal life where each person is united with all his brothers and sisters in praising God the Father, Son, and Holy Spirit forever in heaven.

REFERENCES

Mt 3:17, 17:5

For Reflection

- How is my family a reflection of the Trinity?
- Do I model the self-giving love of God in my relations within my own family?
- How do I pour myself out in love for others?

CONCLUSION

Jesus

"You shall call his name Jesus, for he will save his people from their sins."

How often the history of the world has turned on a single event. The vision of a cross in the sky led to the establishment of a Christian empire. The posting of 95 theses on a Church door initiated the splintering of Western Christendom. And the assassination of Archduke Ferdinand launched World War I and much of the bloodshed of the twentieth century. But one of the greatest turning points of human history occurred when a man tending his flock of sheep stumbled upon the sight of a bush that was burning but not consumed. The fate of the human race was, in this one event, altered irrevocably. Moses' encounter with the one true God led to the creation of the Hebrew nation, a nation which has impacted the world far more than its modest size might lead one to believe.

From the burning bush, God calls Moses to be the leader who will bring the Hebrews out of the bondage of slavery in Egypt. Moses, less than enthusiastic about this momentous task, objects repeatedly to God's plans. One of his objections regards the identity of the one who is calling him:

> "If I come to the people of Israel and say to them, 'The God of your fathers has sent me to you,' and they ask me, 'What is his name?' what shall I say to them?"
>
> — Ex 3:13

Before this encounter, Moses believed that there were many national gods, and he knew that the Israelites would want to know which one was directing him. Furthermore, in the ancient world, knowing a person's name was believed to carry with it great power over that person. If someone knew the true name of a god, he had some authority over that god. Moses hoped that by knowing this god's name, he would gain some control over the deity: this god would be at the beck and call of his people.

God's answer, however, is one of the great revelations in the history of religion. he does not give a name; instead:

> God said to Moses, "I AM WHO AM." And he said, "Say this to the people of Israel, 'I AM has sent me to you.'"
>
> — Ex 3:14

This God is existence itself: there is no beginning or end to him. He has no dependencies — reality itself is based completely in him, and no name can contain him. He *is*.

Although the Jewish people applied the Hebrew word behind "I AM" — "Yahweh" — as God's name, the truth is that God was not giving his name to Moses, but was revealing himself as the true creator and sustainer of all that is. In addition to the "name" *Yahweh,* the Israelites were expansive in all the titles they gave to God over the centuries; they called him the "Judge of all the earth" (Gen 18:25), "Everlasting God" (Gen 21:33), "Holy One of Israel" (Is 1:4), "King of the nations" (Jer 10:7), and "rock, fortress and deliverer" (Ps 18:2). But all of these were titles to describe him, not a name that would reflect an intimate knowledge of another.

This is what names do: they reflect, in a unique way, the sum total of a person. When a father hears the name of his child, he immediately recalls all that is the essence of that child. The very name represents everything about that child in the mind of the father — things good and bad, expressible and inexpressible. It doesn't take long after the birth of a child for the infant's name to be so intimately linked to him that the idea of changing the name is usually unthinkable. Calling someone by name thus forms an intimate link with him or her.

But throughout Old Testament times, God does not reveal himself by a true name, one that is more than a title or description of who he is. Although he cares for his people and guides them, in a real sense, he remains remote in his namelessness. But all that changes, as recorded in the very first chapter of the first book of the New Testament, when an angel announces to Joseph:

> "Joseph, son of David, do not fear to take Mary your wife, for that which is conceived in her is of the Holy Spirit; she will bear a son, and you shall call his name Jesus, for he will save his people from their sins."

> — Mt 1:20-21

This child, conceived by the Holy Spirit, will descend into the human race and will become like man in all things, including having a name. Note also that the angel does not tell Joseph "You shall name him Jesus," but "You shall call his name Jesus." It is not Joseph who names Jesus, but God himself. As the true Father, God has the right to name his child, and from all the names of the world, God chose this one to identify his Son.

The name "Jesus" represents the fundamental reality of the Incarnation: no longer is God content to rule us from eternity. Now, he becomes one of us and opens himself up to us, granting us an intimate relationship that only a name can give. Jesus is not simply a description of who he is or a title of what he does; it is the very name taken by God the Son. This has changed forever how God relates to the world. Although he still cannot be controlled by man, God has subjected himself to be available to us in intimate ways unimaginable before the Incarnation. He makes himself available especially in the sacraments, particularly in the sacraments of Reconciliation and the Eucharist. This is the availability one only finds in a close friend — and friends always call each other by name.

> "No longer do I call you servants, for the servant does not know what his master is doing; but I have called you friends."
>
> — Jn 15:15

A faithful friend is always available when called, and Jesus is the most faithful of friends. Each time a priest celebrates Mass, Jesus humbly comes under the appearance of bread and wine. Whenever the sacrament of confession is celebrated, Jesus is there, pouring forth God's mercy and forgiveness. He has made himself available to his friends in a multitude of ways; even if we are unfaithful, he is faithful, always there to console and comfort us.

But why the name "Jesus" and not some other name? Why not a name like "Michael," which means "who resembles God," or "David," meaning "beloved"? Why is this name above all other names given to the Son of God? The angel tells Joseph that the child's name is Jesus "for he will save his people from their sins" (Mt 1:21). The name Jesus (or, in another form, Joshua) means "Yahweh is salvation." Every human heart recognizes the need for salvation, and our salvation has one object: God himself. Salvation is the presence of God in our lives, God with us — Emmanuel. Jesus is the agent of this salvation; he is the redeemer and deliverer of all men. And the angel explains that what man needs salvation from is his sin. By being the agent who saves us from our sins, Jesus' true identity is revealed, as Blessed Theophylact explains:

> Hence it is clear that it is God Who will be born, for it is the attribute of God alone to forgive sins.
>
> — *Explanation of the Holy Gospel According to St. Matthew*[39]

God, who is the object of salvation, also becomes the means of that salvation in Jesus.

The name "Jesus" was a common one in the time of Christ and throughout the Old Testament, but the angel's words reflect that this was no common man. There is no other Jesus than Jesus of Nazareth. Even the greatest "Jesus" of the Old Testament — Joshua, son of Nun — is but a shadow of the true Jesus. Joshua defeated the enemies of Israel and delivered the people of God into the Promised Land. Jesus defeated far greater enemies — Satan, sin, and death — and delivers the new people of God — the Church — into the promised land of heaven.

A beautiful icon of Holy Saturday depicts Christ's descent into Hades. In this image, Jesus stands on gates representing the crushed Gates of Hades, trampling on death itself. His brilliance overwhelms the abyss. Christ is reaching down and grabbing the hands of Adam and Eve, pulling them from their imprisonment in the pit so that he can take them to their eternal home in heaven. Adam and Eve are the first among the many righteous men and women residing in the bosom of Abraham awaiting the salvation of Christ. One can just imagine Joshua, son of Nun, rejoicing at the arrival of the true Salvation into the darkness of death.

A great devotion to the Holy Name of Jesus arose in the Middle Ages, fostered by saints such as St. John Capistran and St. Bernardine of Siena. But it was St. Bernard of Clairvaux who, cultivating this devotion in the Church in the eleventh century, elaborated upon the benefits that flow from this name:

> The Name of Jesus is Light, and Food, and Medicine. It is Light, when it is preached to us; it is Food, when we think upon it; it is the Medicine that soothes our pains when we invoke it . . . There is nothing which so restrains the impulse of anger, calms the swelling of pride, heals the wound of envy, represses the insatiability of luxury, smothers the flame of lust, quenches the thirst of avarice, and dispels the fever of uncleanliness — as the Name of Jesus. For when I pronounce this Name, I bring before my mind the Man, who, by excellence, is meek and

humble of heart, benign, sober, chaste, merciful, and filled with everything that is good and holy, nay, who is the very God Almighty — whose example heals me, and whose assistance strengthens me. I say all this, when I say Jesus. Here have I my model, for he is Man; and my help, for he is God; the one provides me with precious drugs, the other gives them efficacy; and from the two I make potion such as no physician knows how to make.

— *Fifteenth Sermon on the Canticle of Canticles*[40]

As part of the devotion to the holy name of Jesus, the monogram "IHS" (representing the Latinized first three letters of the Greek version of *Jesus*) was promoted as an emblem of the faith. It was placed over the gates of a city to call upon the protection of the Lord and on garments to remind the wearer of his Savior. The founder of the Jesuits, St. Ignatius of Loyola, made this monogram the emblem of his order. The promoters of this devotion understood the power of this name — not by virtue of some magical capacity belonging to the letters, but because the divine Savior had taken this name above all other names in his work of redemption.

The name Jesus is central to the Christian faith: it contains great power and authority, it is the door of salvation, and it is the center of prayer. By taking the name Jesus, the Lord has conferred on it great authority and power. St. Paul writes:

God exalted him and bestowed on him the name which is above every name, that at the name of Jesus every knee should bow, in heaven and on earth and under the earth.

— Phil 2:9-10

The very name Jesus is able now to make demons flee and convert hearts to God. It is the name by which all men are saved, as St. Peter proclaimed to all who would listen:

> "There is salvation in no one else, for there is no other name under heaven given among men by which we must be saved."
>
> — Acts 4:12

The name of the gate to heaven is Jesus; only through that name has salvation come to the human race. This is the name that the Church preaches and the name in which it does everything.

> The name of Jesus is at the heart of Christian prayer. All liturgical prayers conclude with the words "through our Lord Jesus Christ." The *Hail Mary* reaches its high point in the words "blessed is the fruit of thy womb, Jesus." The Eastern prayer of the heart, the *Jesus Prayer*, says: "Lord Jesus Christ, Son of God, have mercy on me, a sinner." Many Christians, such as St. Joan of Arc, have died with the one word "Jesus" on their lips.
>
> — *CCC* 435

Everything the Christian does is centered on the name of Jesus. Never will anyone be disappointed who trusts in this great name, because the one who bears it promised to hear and respond to any plea made in his name. The name Jesus is, in and of itself, a perfect prayer; in the fact that God became a man — Jesus — lies all our hope.

There is no name more exalted than the name of Jesus. He is the Son of God, the Christ, Lord, teacher, prophet, and much else besides. But above all, he is Jesus, our Salvation.

REFERENCES

Mt 1:21, 25

For Reflection

- How often is the name of Jesus on my lips and in my heart?
- In my life do I proclaim, to the glory of the Father, that Jesus is Lord?

ENDNOTES

1. Simonetti, Manlio, ed. *Ancient Christian Commentary on Scripture, New Testament Ia: Matthew 1-13 (ACCSNTIa)*. Downers Grove, IL: InterVarsity Press, 2001, p. 169.

2. Ibid. *Ib: Matthew 14-28 (ACCSNTIb)*. Downers Grove, IL: InterVarsity Press, 2002, pp. 246-247.

3. *ACCSNTIa*, p. 246.

4. Menzies, Allan, ed. *Ante-Nicene Fathers, Volume 9*. Peabody, MA: Hendrickson Publishers, Inc., 1994, p. 341.

5. Just, Arthur, Jr., ed. *Ancient Christian Commentary on Scripture, New Testament III: Luke (ACCSNTIII)*. Downers Grove, IL: InterVarsity Press, 2003, p. 63.

6. *ACCSNTIa*, pp. 39-40.

7. Schaff, Philip, and Henry Wace, eds. *Nicene and Post-Nicene Fathers, Second Series, Volume 13*. Peabody, MA: Hendrickson Publishers, Inc., 1994, p. 398.

8. Kavanaugh, Kieran, O.C.D., trans. *The Collected Works of St. John of the Cross*. Washington, DC: ICS Publications, 1991, p. 216.

9. *ACCSNTIb*, p. 44.

10. Schaff and Wace, eds. *Nicene and Post-Nicene Fathers, Second Series, Volume 1*. Peabody, MA: Hendrickson Publishers, Inc., 1994, p. 89.

11. Kavanaugh, Kieran, O.C.D., trans. *The Collected Works of St. Teresa of Avila, Volume Two*. Washington, DC: ICS Publications, 1980, p. 117.

12. Palmer, G.E.H., Philip Sherrard, and Kallistos Ware, trans. *The Philokalia: The Complete Text, Volume 1*. London: Faber and Faber, 1979, p. 318.

13. Roberts, Alexander, and James Donaldson, eds. *Ante-Nicene Fathers, Volume 1 (ANFI)*. Peabody, MA: Hendrickson Publishers, Inc., 1994, p. 186.

14. Schaff and Wace, eds. *Nicene and Post-Nicene Fathers, Second Series, Volume 8*. Peabody, MA: Hendrickson Publishers, Inc., 1994, p. 65.

15. Bonhoeffer, Dietrich. *The Cost of Discipleship*. New York: Simon and Schuster, 1995, p. 91.

16. Author's own translation.

17. *ACCSNTIb*, pp. 290-291.

18. *ACCSNTIa*, p. 159.

19. Ibid., p. 37.

20. Ibid. p. 38.

21. *ANFI*, pp. 89-90, slightly edited by author.

22. Chadwick, Henry, trans. *Confessions of St. Augustine*. Oxford: Oxford University Press, 2008, p. 3.

23. Roberts and Donaldson, eds. *Ante-Nicene Fathers, Volume 2*. Peabody, MA: Hendrickson Publishers, Inc., 1994, p. 210.

24. *ACCSNTIb*, p. 146.

25. Vollert, Cyril, trans. *Compendium of Theology*. B. Herder Book Co., 1947, p. 1.

26. Palmer, Sherrard, and Ware, trans. *Philokalia: the Eastern Christian Spiritual Txts: Selections Annotated & Explained*. Woodstock, VT: SkyLight Paths Publishing, 2008, p. 201.

27. Chadwick, p. 124.

28. ANFI, p. 163.

29. Sheridan, Mark, ed. *Ancient Christian Commentary on Scripture, Old Testament, Volume II*. Downers Grove, IL: InterVarsity Press, 2002, p. 105.

30. Pope Pius XI, *Quas Primas*. http://www.vatican.va/holy_father/pius_xi/encyclicals/documents/hf_p-xi_enc_11121925_quas-primas_en.html.

31. Theological Students Fellowship. *Themelios, Volumes 10-11*. British Theological Students' Fellowship and International Fellowship of Evangelical Students, 1984, p. 9.

32. Quoted in Pius XI, *Quas Primas*.

33. *Quas Primas*.

34. *ACCSNTIb*, p. 161.

35. Quoted in Ware, Timothy. *The Orthodox Church*. Middlesex, England: Penguin Books, 1963, p. 41.

36. *ACCSNTIa*, p. 54.

37. Quoted in Hahn, Scott. *First Comes Love*. New York: Image Books, 2002, p. 42.

38. Roberts and Donaldson, eds. *Ante-Nicene Christian Library: The writings of Cyprian I*. T. and T. Clark, 1868, p. 403.

39. Stade, Fr. Christopher, trans. *The Explanation by Blessed Theophylact of the Holy Gospel According to Saint Matthew*. House Springs, MO: Chrysostom Press, 2006, p. 20.

40. Quoted in Guéranger, Prosper. *The Liturgical Year, Volume 2*. Burns and Oats, 1904, pp. 260-262.